The Eucharistic Celebration

The Source and Summit of Faith

Adolf Adam

The Eucharistic Celebration

The Source
and Summit of Faith

Translated by Robert C. Schultz

A PUEBLO BOOK

The Liturgical Press   Collegeville, Minnesota

The Eucharistic Celebration: The Source and Summit of Faith is the authorized English translation of *Die Eucharistiefeier: Quelle und Gipfel des Glaubens,* published by Herder Verlag, Freiburg im Breisgau, 1991. The publisher of this English edition has adapted the liturgical texts and commentary to conform to current official usage in the United States.

The Scripture quotations contained herein are from the New Revised Standard Version of the Bible: Catholic Edition © 1993 and 1989 by the Division of Christian Education of the National Council of the Churches of Christ in the U.S.A. Used by permission. All rights reserved.

Excerpts from the English translation of *The Roman Missal* © 1973, International Committee on English in the Liturgy, Inc. (ICEL); excerpts from the English translation of *Lectionary for Mass* © 1969, ICEL; excerpts from the English translation of the *General Instruction of the Roman Missal;* the *Directory for Masses with Children;* the *General Norms for the Liturgical Year and Calendar;* the apostolic constitution *Missale Romanum;* the circular letter *Eucharistiae Participationem;* and the instructions *Eucharisticum Mysterium, Immensae Caritatis,* and *Actio Pastoralis* are from *Documents on the Liturgy, 1963–1979: Conciliar, Papal, and Curial Texts* © 1982, ICEL. All rights reserved.

Excerpts from the English translation of the Constitution on the Sacred Liturgy (*Sacrosanctum Concilium*), the Dogmatic Constitution on the Church (*Lumen Gentium*), and the Dogmatic Constitution on Divine Revelation (*Dei Verbum*) are taken from *Vatican Council II: The Conciliar and Post Conciliar Documents,* ed. Austin Flannery, O.P., rev. ed. (Collegeville, Minn.: The Liturgical Press, 1992).

Designed by Frank Kacmarcik, Obl.S.B.

Printed in the United States of America.

Library of Congress Cataloging-in-Publication Data

Adam, Adolf, 1912-
    [Eucharistiefeier. English]
    The Eucharistic celebration : the source and summit of faith /
  Adolf Adam ; translated by Robert C. Schultz.
       p.   cm.
    Translation of: Die Eucharistiefeier.
    ''A Pueblo book.''
    Includes bibliographical references.
    ISBN 0-8146-6123-8
    1. Mass. 2. Lord's Supper (Liturgy) 3. Lord's Supper—Catholic
  Church. 4. Catholic Church—Liturgy. 5. Catholic Church-
  -Doctrines. I. Title.
    BX2230.2.A3213 1994
264'.02036—dc20   94-757
                                                  CIP

Contents

CHAPTER THREE
Special Forms of the Celebration of the Mass   123

CHAPTER FOUR
Sunday and the Eucharistic Celebration   132

Preface

Current regard for the value of the sacred Mass, measured in terms of what people think of it as well as of their level of participation in it, is very low in general. Many factors have contributed to this situation. Here we need draw attention only to the widespread loss of the awareness of transcendence in modern society. As a result, there is a sense of indifference to, and growing ignorance of, the Christian faith.

This fact has particularly affected the Church's worship. The Second Vatican Council asserted that this worship is "the fount from which all [the Church's] power flows" and "the summit toward which the activity of the Church is directed" (SC 10). Referring specifically to the Eucharistic celebration, the Council describes participation in the Eucharistic sacrifice as the "source and summit of the Christian life" (LG 11). The assertion of the wise Greek philosopher Socrates that whoever knows the good also does it certainly does not apply to everyone. And yet the "quiet power of the truth" (Romano Guardini) still works effectively today. There are still people today whose choice of lifestyle is determined by their knowledge of the truth. This fact is the basis of the author's hope that appreciation of the Mass might once again rise if the barriers that prevent people from making use of the Mass are removed and if the meaning and value of the Mass become better known again.

The present book is intended to provide the knowledge, insights, and impulses that are needed for this to happen. Although the book rests on secure scholarly foundations, it forgoes providing an extensive "scholarly apparatus" so that it may reach a broader group of readers. For the sake of these readers, it attempts to use understandable terminology and a form of presentation that will provide insight into the value and meaning of the celebration of the Mass. It is also intended to deepen Eucharistic faith and to provide an aid for the transmission of this faith in family and group discussions, in catechetical instruction, and in preaching.

We intentionally avoid proposing further reforms of the liturgy. After the numerous changes in the liturgy that resulted from the Second Vatican Council, the celebration of the Eucharist now needs a period of more thorough instruction and reflection. Only after such a period should further improvements be undertaken, such as trying to achieve a legitimate integration of the liturgy with contemporary culture.

This book begins with three sections providing basic information. The first deals with the institution of the Eucharist and the historical records that describe this institution. The second section contains a necessarily brief description of the most important historical developments of the celebration of the Mass, for the present situation can be better understood only with some knowledge of the historical development. The third section provides information about the conciliar and postconciliar reforms of the Mass and explains the basic goals of these reforms.

The main section of the book lays out the structure of the Mass and focuses on its individual elements. In doing so, it often seemed necessary to bring out the meaning and richness of the ancient symbols and symbolic actions for modern people so that their message can be heard. The primary concern of this section is to explore the theological and spiritual depths of the celebration of Mass and to illuminate their relationship to the Christian life. For it is only initiation into the Christ-mystery (mystagogy) that makes possible a truly Christian existence.

Following the main section, some special forms of the Mass are described. A concluding section focuses on the problems associated with the theme "Sunday and the Eucharistic Celebration."

This book, then, seeks to contribute to the goal set by the Second Vatican Council:

"The Church, therefore, earnestly desires that Christ's faithful, when present at this mystery of faith, should not be there as strangers or silent spectators. On the contrary, through a good understanding of the rites and prayers they should take part in the sacred action, conscious of what they are doing, with devotion and full collaboration. They should be instructed by God's word and be nourished at the table of the Lord's Body. They should give thanks to God'' (*SC* 48).

ADOLF ADAM

Mainz
Easter 1991

Translator's Note

I wish to thank the Seattle University Library as well as the Office of Worship and Sacraments of the Archdiocese of Seattle for permission to use materials in their collections. Carolyn Lassek, director of the archdiocesan office, and her administrative assistant, Katy Callaghan Houston, assisted me in locating a number of sources.

At a later stage in the development of this translation, Dr. James J. Megivern of the University of North Carolina in Wilmington performed the friendly service of reading the manuscript and suggesting a number of revisions that have made it more readable. I also wish to thank Mr. John Schneider of The Liturgical Press for his careful editing of the translation. I, of course, remain responsible for any inaccuracies in the translation. In the preparation of the English text, specific references to the unique characteristics of the German text have usually been omitted.

R.C.S.

Abbreviations

AAS	*Acta Apostolicae Sedis*
DMC	Directory for Masses with Children. *DOL*, pp. 676–688.
DOL	*Documents on the Liturgy, 1963–1979: Conciliar, Papal and Curial Texts* (Collegeville, Minn.: The Liturgical Press, 1982).
DV	*Dei Verbum*, Dogmatic Constitution on Divine Revelation. *Flannery* 1:750–765.
Gemeinsame Synode	*Gemeinsame Synode der Bistümer in der Bundes-republik Deutschland*, Vol. I: *Beschlüsse der Vollver-sammlung. Offizielle Gesamtausgabe* (Würzburg), 7th ed. (Freiburg: Herder, 1989): *Gottesdienst* ["Worship"].
German Missal	*Messbuch für die Bistümer des deutschen Sprachge-bietes. Kleinausgabe. Das Messbuch deutsch für alle Tage des Jahres*, 2nd ed. (Freiburg: Herder, 1988).
GIRM	General Instruction of the Roman Missal. *DOL*, pp. 465–533.
GNLYC	General Norms for the Liturgical Year and the Calendar. *DOL*, pp. 1155–1167.
Gottesdienst	*Gottesdienst. Information und Handreichung der liturgischen Institut* (Liturgical Institutes: Salzburg—Trier—Zürich).
Gotteslob	*Gotteslob. Katholisches Gebet- und Gesangbuch* . . . The German hymnal *Gotteslob* is published in various diocesan editions. The liturgical section and songs 1–791 are the same in all these edi-

tions. A specific diocesan edition will be noted for references to nos. 792 and above.

LD	*The Liturgy Documents: A Parish Resource,* 3rd ed. (Chicago: Liturgy Training Publications, 1991).
Lectionary	*Lectionary for Mass* (Collegeville, Minn.: The Liturgical Press, 1970).
LG	*Lumen Gentium,* Dogmatic Constitution on the Church. *Flannery* 1:350–423.
LMIn	*Lectionary for Mass: Introduction,* 2nd typical edition, 1981 (Collegeville, Minn.: The Liturgical Press, 1986).
RM	*The Roman Missal* (Collegeville, Minn.: The Liturgical Press, 1974, 1985).
Rites	*The Rites of the Catholic Church.* Vol. 2 (Collegeville, Minn.: The Liturgical Press, 1991).
SC	*Sacrosanctum Concilium,* Constitution on the Sacred Liturgy. *Flannery* 1:1-36.
WL	*Worship and Liturgy,* ed. James J. Megivern (Wilmington, N.C.: McGrath, 1978).

Chapter One

Basic Information

INSTITUTION: THE HISTORICAL EVENT AND ITS RECORDS
On the evening before his Passion, Jesus and his disciples shared a solemn meal. Modern research confirms the traditional understanding that it was probably the Passover meal, which was celebrated at the beginning of the Jewish Passover festival.[1] This festival, celebrated on the evening before the first full moon of spring, continues to be extremely significant in the life of Jews up to the present time. It is a meal in commemoration of God's saving activity in the Exodus from Egypt, in their wonderful and saving passage through the Sea of Reeds (Red Sea), and in their wandering through the wilderness before they entered the Promised Land.

During this ritual meal, which consisted of unleavened bread, bitter herbs steeped in a fruit sauce (*charoset*) before the meal, and the Passover lamb, three goblets of wine (later four) were blessed and distributed to the participants in their own drinking glasses. During the meal the head of the family responded to the questions asked by the youngest participant by telling the story of Israel's liberation from Egypt (this narrative is called the "Haggadah"). It was explicitly emphasized that these saving acts of God were not merely historical events experienced by their ancestors but were also to be understood as re-presenting God's same saving faithfulness to his covenant with those now partaking of

[1] A detailed overview of recent scholarly research is provided by Hans Bernhard Meyer and Irmgard Pahl, "*Eucharistie. Geschichte, Theologie, Pastoral*" in *Gottesdienst der Kirche. Handbuch der Liturgiewissenschaft*, vol. 4, ed. Hans Bernhard Meyer and Hansjörg Maur, (Regensburg: F. Pustet, 1989), pp. 61–68.

this meal. Thus the Haggadah text used today during this meal contains the following statement:

"In each generation, every individual should feel as though he or she had actually been redeemed from Mitzrayim [Egypt], as it is said 'You shall tell your children on that day, saying, "It is because of what Adonai did for me when I went free out of Mitzrayim"' (Exodus 13:8). For the Holy One redeemed not only our ancestors; He redeemed us with them, as it is said, 'He brought us out of there, so that He might bring us to the land He promised our ancestors'" (Deut 6:23).[2]

It was in this context that Jesus as the Son of God, one in being with this God who acts to save his people, instituted the new covenant meal of the Eucharistic sacrament. The New Testament describes this event in four places. Because of the fundamental significance of this event, we give here these four descriptions.

Matthew 26:26-28
"While they were eating, Jesus took a loaf of bread, and after blessing it he broke it, gave it to the disciples, and said, 'Take, eat; this is my body.' Then he took a cup, and after giving thanks he gave it to them, saying, 'Drink from it, all of you, for this is my blood of the covenant, which is poured out for many for the forgiveness of sins.'"

Mark 14:22-24
"While they were eating, he took a loaf of bread, and after blessing it he broke it, gave it to them, and said, 'Take; this is my body.' Then he took a cup, and after giving thanks he gave it to them, and all of them drank from it. He said to them, 'This is my blood of the covenant, which is poured out for many.'"

Luke 22:19-20
"Then he took a loaf of bread, and when he had given thanks, he broke it and gave it to them, saying, 'This is my body, which is

[2] Rachel Anne Rabinowicz, ed., *Passover Haggadah: The Feast of Freedom*, 2nd ed. (The Rabbinical Assembly, 1982), p. 67. See Theodore H. Gaster, *Festivals of the Jewish Year: A Modern Interpretation and Guide* (New York: William Morrow and Co., 1953), pp. 42f.

2

given for you. Do this in remembrance of me.' And he did the
same with the cup after supper, saying, 'This cup that is poured
out for you is the new covenant in my blood.' "

1 Corinthians 11:23-26
"For I received from the Lord what I also handed on to you, that
the Lord Jesus on the night when he was betrayed took a loaf of
bread, and when he had given thanks, he broke it and said,
'This is my body that is for you. Do this in remembrance of me.'
In the same way he took the cup also, after supper, saying, 'This
cup is the new covenant in my blood. Do this, as often as you
drink it, in remembrance of me.' For as often as you eat this
bread and drink the cup, you proclaim the Lord's death until
he comes."

Although the Gospel of John does not report the institution of the
Eucharist, it does describe the promise and meaning of the bread
of heaven that is Jesus himself:

John 6:48-58
" 'I am the bread of life. Your ancestors ate the manna in the
wilderness, and they died. This is the bread that comes down
from heaven, so that one may eat of it and not die. I am the living bread that came down from heaven. Whoever eats of this
bread will live forever; and the bread that I will give for the life
of the world is my flesh.'

"The Jews then disputed among themselves, saying, 'How can
this man give us his flesh to eat?' So Jesus said to them, 'Very
truly, I tell you, unless you eat the flesh of the Son of Man and
drink his blood, you have no life in you. Those who eat my flesh
and drink my blood have eternal life, and I will raise them up on
the last day; for my flesh is true food and my blood is true drink.
Those who eat my flesh and drink my blood abide in me, and I in
them. Just as the living Father sent me, and I live because of the
Father, so whoever eats me will live because of me. This is the
bread that came down from heaven, not like that which your ancestors ate, and they died. But the one who eats this bread will
live forever.' "

3

If we consider these sources and summarize their common content in a single statement, we arrive at the following: During his Last Supper, Jesus presented bread and wine to his disciples and made these decisive statements to interpret what he was doing: "This is my body" and "This is my blood." The accompanying statements make it clear that he was speaking of his sacrificed body and his blood shed as a sacrifice. They are sacrificed and shed "for you," "for many."

Jesus intentionally chose bread and wine as signs of the redeeming sacrifice of his body and blood, for bread and wine are means of sustaining life; they give joy and strength, and when shared in a common meal, they create fellowship. Thus these natural elements of the meal already indicate the effects of the Eucharistic meal: life, strength, joy, and fellowship. This meal does all this because it joins us to, and unites us with, the redeeming Lord. To be one with Jesus means that we are also one with his submission to the Father's will, one with his love and readiness to sacrifice himself for the salvation of people, one with his intention to glorify his heavenly Father and to give true life to people in all that he did.

Whoever receives this Eucharistic food actually becomes objectively one with Christ. However, the subjective appropriation of this reality that permits a person to join with all truthfulness in Paul's confession "It is no longer I who live, but it is Christ who lives in me" (Gal 2:20) remains a task to be worked on through all of life. Paul's assertion becomes subjectively true for us as we make room for Christ and his word to develop their meaning in our thoughts and actions.

The Eucharistic meal is also intended to lead us into fellowship with other people, beginning with those who are also united with Christ through it. All who are united with Christ are also joined with one another. This means that no partaker of the meal may treat another partaker like a stranger or deal with him or her in a loveless manner. Unity with Christ becomes unity with one another. "Because there is one bread, we who are many are one body, for we all partake of the one bread" (1 Cor 10:17).

In two places (Luke 22:19; 1 Cor 11:24-25), the historical records of the institution contain the Lord's instruction to continue re-enacting this meal in the future, and to do so "in remembrance" of him. Whenever a Christian community gathers together to celebrate the Eucharist, they do not merely remember the past; rather, he who sacrificed himself for the salvation of the world is present as the living Lord. The early Christian Church understood this and acted accordingly (see 1 Cor 10:16f.; 11:26).

Frequently in history stone monuments have been erected as memorials for people who have sacrificed themselves for others. The "memorial monument" for Christ's redemptive self-sacrifice is this life-giving meal. In this meal he continues to carry out his basic assertion: "I came that they may have life, and have it abundantly" (John 10:10). This Eucharistic meal is the new paradisiacal "tree of life" that now stands in the center of the garden of our life. We are told that no one was to eat the fruit of the tree of life in the Garden of Eden or even to touch it (see Gen 2:9; 3:3). No such prohibition is posted in front of the Eucharistic tree of life; rather, there is an invitation and a promise: "Those who eat my flesh and drink my blood have eternal life, and I will raise them up on the last day" (John 6:54).

For those who think about what this really means, the celebration of the Mass will become a Eucharist, that is, a great act of thanksgiving. The Jewish Passover meal was already a joyous act of praise for God's wonderful works in creation and in Israel's salvation history. The Eucharistic celebration gives thanks for these, too, but primarily it gives thanks for the mystery of our redemption in Christ—the paschal mystery. This thanksgiving is not only focused on the past and the present but is also directed toward the future consummation of salvation that Christ has promised us through this sacrament (see above, John 6:54).

Thus when Christians celebrate the Eucharist, they experience themselves as loved by the triune God in a manner that is beyond their understanding. And they know that they are held safely in this love both in the present and for the future, even though their life is threatened from within and without.

It is easy to understand that this basic structure of the Eucharistic celebration has both preserved its essential elements and assumed various cultural forms. The Church itself has grown into a world-wide fellowship of faith, and in this process the Eucharistic celebration has been immersed in various cultural environments. The changing spirituality of people from one age of history to another has also left its marks in the form of an emphasis on elements that were especially relevant to people at a particular time. A description of these developments would fill many thick volumes.[3]

In this book we shall attempt to describe only the most important lines of development in a very concise form and without scholarly references to the literature. This brief description will focus primarily on the Roman rite, the *Missa Romana*, which has been the dominant form in the Western world.

In the apostolic communities the Eucharistic meal was usually combined with a meal that satisfied hunger (the Agape). This Agape meal was gradually discontinued not only because of the growing abuses at this meal (see 1 Cor 11:17-34) but also because of the rapidly growing membership of the communities. The many tables needed for a meal that satisfied hunger were replaced by the one "holy table" of the Eucharist.

About the year 150, Justin Martyr, a Christian philosopher from Antioch, gave us the first complete description of the Eucharistic celebration as it was observed in Rome and other parts of the Church. He tells us that the Eucharist itself was preceded by a service of the Word with intercessions:

"On the day named after the sun, people who live in the cities and in the country gather for a common celebration. Then the

[3] For example, Hans B. Meyer and Irmgard Pahl, *Eucharistie. Geschichte, Theologie, Pastoral*, and Josef A. Jungmann, *Missarum Sollemnia*, 2 vols. (Freiburg: Herder, 1960). An abridged one-volume translation of Jungmann's work is available in English: *The Mass of the Roman Rite: Its Origins and Development*, trans. Francis A. Brunner, rev. Charles K. Riepe (New York: Benziger Brothers, Inc., 1959).

writings that the apostles have left or the writings of the prophets are read, as long as time allows. After the reader finishes his task, the president gives an address in which he urgently admonishes the people to follow these excellent teachings in their lives. Then we all stand up together and offer prayers. After the end of the prayers, . . . bread, wine, and water are brought and the president offers up prayers and thanksgiving—as much as he is able. The people assent by speaking 'Amen.' Then the things over which thanks has been said are distributed to all who are present, and the deacons take some to those who are absent. In addition, those who are well-to-do give whatever they wish. Whatever is collected is kept by the president, who uses it to help widows and orphans'' (*First Apology*, chap. 67).

In describing the Eucharist, Justin explicitly bases his understanding on the teaching of the apostles contained in the Gospels:

''We call this food the 'Eucharist.' No one may share in it who does not believe that our teaching is true and who has not been washed in the bath of baptism that results in the forgiveness of sins and in rebirth to a new life. We do not consume these gifts as though they were common bread or drink. For according to our teaching, as our Redeemer Jesus Christ has become flesh through the divine Logos and for the sake of our salvation has assumed our flesh and blood, it is our teaching that through our prayer to the Logos . . . this food and drink that have been dedicated through prayer also become the body and blood of this Jesus, which in turn transform and nourish our flesh and blood. For in the writings left by the apostles, which we call 'Gospels,' they report that they received the following command: Jesus took bread, gave thanks, and said: 'Do this to remember me; this is my body.' In the same way, he took the cup, gave thanks, and said: 'This is my blood' '' (*First Apology*, chap. 66).

The first example of a Eucharistic Prayer is found in Hippolytus' *Apostolic Tradition*, written about 225.[4] It begins with the dialogue

[4] *The Treatise on the Apostolic Tradition of St. Hippolytus of Rome, Bishop and Martyr*, ed. Gregory Dix; reissued with corrections, preface, and bibli-

and the preface (iv, 3ff.), as is still the custom today, and ends with the great doxology that precedes the Lord's Prayer. The current Eucharistic Prayers of the Roman Missal, written after the Second Vatican Council and published in 1969–70, adopt this Eucharistic Prayer, which has been described as "a Eucharistic Prayer from the time of the martyrs,"[5] with some changes and adjustments, as Eucharistic Prayer II. This demonstrates the continuity of the process that shaped the liturgy of the Mass. Hippolytus, who understood himself as a representative of the conservative movement, explicitly emphasized that his text of the Eucharistic Prayer was only a model. The individual celebrant was not required to use it word for word but did have to maintain the basic outline of the text.

Accordingly, the later Roman liturgy did not simply adopt Hippolytus' text word for word but rather recast and expanded it. Many of these changes occurred during the transition from Greek to Latin as the basic language of the liturgy. Popes Leo I (440–461), Gelasius I (492–496), and Gregory the Great (590–604) were the most influential in shaping the Roman liturgy.

In the seventh century a far-reaching process of merging the Roman with the Gaulish-Frankish liturgies that had developed north of the Alps began. Many elements of these Gaulish-Frankish liturgies began to be included in the Roman liturgy, including the Roman Mass. This can be seen, for example, in the preference for dramatic forms, for more numerous and longer prayers and liturgies, and for many silent prayers on the part of the celebrant. Toward the end of the eighth century, the custom of speaking the Eucharistic Prayer very softly was introduced. The understanding of the Mass was now determined by the "allegorical explanation of the Mass." Deeper meaning was seen behind every liturgical detail, often based on artificial interpretations that were far re-

---

ography by Henry Chadwick (London: The Alban Press, 1992 [1st ed., 1937; 2nd rev. ed., 1968]), iv, 1–13 (pp. 6–9).

[5] See Theodor Schnitzler, *Die drei neuen eucharistischen Hochgebete und die neuen Präfationen. In Verkündigung und Betrachtung,* (Freiburg: Herder, 1968), p. 25.

moved from the liturgy itself. Medieval people had an unusually strong consciousness of unworthiness and sinfulness. This fact resulted in the adoption of numerous broadly formulated confessions of sin in the literature of prayer and especially in the liturgy of the Mass.

These transformations of the Roman liturgy of the Mass reached Rome in the tenth and eleventh centuries through numerous manuscripts. At that time religious and cultural life in Rome had reached its lowest point, and few manuscripts were produced there. So it was that what had once been the Roman liturgy came back to Rome in a Gaulish-Frankish form. This transformed liturgy was considered to be the "liturgy of the Roman Curia" and now began its triumphal march as the universal liturgy of the West. It was Pope Gregory VII (1073–1085) and later the Franciscan Order that brought about the almost universal adoption of this form of the liturgy.

During the Gothic period new energies and forms entered into worship. Up until then the liturgy had always been understood and celebrated as a communal act; now individualistic and subjective tendencies began to appear. "Complete missals" [*Vollmissalien*] enabled a priest to say a private Mass without a lector or a choir, and often even without a congregation. Even the celebrations of the Mass in parishes, cloisters, and religious institutions became liturgies of the clergy; they did everything by themselves, without any active participation of the laity.

As a result, for the simple believer the Mass was covered by two veils. Not only was the Latin language not understandable, but the Eucharistic Prayer and other texts were spoken so softly as to be inaudible. The attention of the laity was focused on the elevation of the host and the chalice at the consecration. The reception of Communion decreased to such an extent that the Fourth Lateran Council (1215) prescribed that everyone was obliged to receive Communion at least once a year. The inflated reverence for the Sacrament also led to the custom of placing the host on the tongue of the communicant rather than in the hand. Communion from the cup fell into disuse. As the lack of understanding of the liturgical event increased, popular piety turned more and more to the veneration of relics, to pilgrimages, to mystery plays, and to the veneration of a specific patron saint for every need.

Not even the Council of Trent (1545–1563) could achieve any thorough reform of the deplorable condition of the liturgy. Because of lack of time, it authorized the Pope, with the assistance of a commission of experts, to prepare new editions of all the liturgical books. Accordingly, the Roman Breviary was published in 1568 and the Roman Missal in 1570. The Sacred Congregation of Rites was established in 1588 and was authorized to supervise the faithful adoption of the newly ordered liturgies. However, the post-Tridentine liturgy remained "a continuation of the Middle Ages . . . a separate liturgy of the clergy. . . . The language is still Latin. . . . With the exception of the sermon, very little consideration is given to the people of God."[6] The people simply attended Mass, their participation limited to listening and watching. For the common people, the liturgy of the Mass remained a mystery that was hardly even understood.

In the baroque period the official worship of the Church was accompanied by increasingly magnificent displays. The solemn space of the many baroque churches and the polyphonic choirs and instrumental music in the larger churches made the celebration of the Mass a "feast for eyes and ears." The spread of the unfortunate practice of not distributing Communion until after the Mass strengthened the "solitary piety of Communion." The sermon was usually given before the Mass itself and thus was separated from its organic context in the liturgy of the Word. Of this situation Jungmann writes: "A uniquely centripetal force can be recognized in all forms of liturgical life. Medieval developments continue without anyone being concerned about their sources."[7]

---

[6] Josef Jungmann, "Das Konzil von Trient und die Erneuerung der Liturgie," in Georg Schreiber, *Das Weltkonzil von Trient, sein Werden und Wirken,* vol. 1 (Freiburg: Herder, 1951), pp. 329f.

[7] Josef Jungmann, *Liturgisches Erbe und pastoral Gegenwart. Studien und Vorträge* (Innsbruck: Tyrolia, 1960), p. 118.

The new spirituality of the Enlightenment resulted in the strengthening of efforts at reform. People increasingly viewed the liturgy in terms of its usefulness, emphasized its characteristic as a communal act, and strove for greater simplicity and "rationality."

In the romantic movement of the early nineteenth century, the pendulum swung away from the emphases of the Enlightenment, even though the romantic movement was not really concerned with the liturgy. However, the following Catholic Restoration was quite different. This movement, which sought to reestablish close ties to Rome and to the High Middle Ages, largely shaped the Catholic Church in the second half of the nineteenth century and beyond (the modern Scholastic movement, the imitation of the medieval Romanesque and Gothic architectural styles, etc.). It (incorrectly) saw the Roman liturgy as the original Roman form, cultivated it as a venerable value, and attempted to generate enthusiasm for it among the faithful. The Benedictine abbot Prosper Guéranger of Solesmes (1805–1875) is a representative of these efforts. He was particularly involved in the cultivation of Roman or Gregorian chant. Other Benedictine abbeys, such as Beuron and Maria Laach in Germany and Maredsous and Mont César in Belgium, were influenced by the work of Dom Guéranger and his abbey and contributed to the research and promotion of the liturgy.

The first half of the twentieth century experienced the beginning and flowering of the "liturgical movement." We can date its beginning to a document of Pope Pius X, who in 1903 encouraged Catholics "to be present at the Holy Sacrifice of the Altar . . . and to join in the common prayer of the Church in the public and solemn liturgical offices."[8] The great enthusiasm of this movement revealed itself in various ways, especially in the manner in which Mass was celebrated. The *Missa recitata* (i.e., read rather than sung), first celebrated in Maria Laach, developed into the *Gemeinschaftsmesse* (community Mass), the *Betsingmesse* (a prayed and

[8] "*Tra le sollecitudini. Motu proprio* of Pope Pius X on the Restoration of Church Music. November 22, 1903." WL, p. 16.

sung Mass), and the *Volkschoralamt* (the congregational choral Mass) under the leadership of Pius Parsch.

Although the liturgical movement in its first decades focused on the renewed participation of the faithful in the existing Tridentine liturgy, liturgists in the middle of the twentieth century became increasingly aware that the liturgy itself needed reform. Pius XII took a first step with his reform of the Easter Vigil (1951) and his revision of the Holy Week liturgies (1955). This renewal was generally greeted as necessary, meaningful, and pastorally valuable. Thus the time was ripe for further reforms, particularly of the liturgy of the Mass.

THE REFORM OF THE LITURGY OF THE MASS BY VATICAN II
The adoption of the Constitution on the Sacred Liturgy (*SC*) on December 4, 1963, exactly four hundred years after the closing session of the Council of Trent, was a significant event not only for the liturgy but also for the life of the Catholic Church. This was the first document of the Council to be adopted, and the vote was 2147 for and only 4 against. It contains many general statements about, and directions for, the whole liturgical life of the Church (chap. 1). The following selections are of special significance for the Eucharist:

"It is the liturgy through which, especially in the divine sacrifice of the Eucharist, 'the work of our redemption is accomplished' " (*SC* 2).

"The liturgy, then, is rightly seen as an exercise of the priestly office of Jesus Christ. It involves the presentation of man's sanctification under the guise of signs perceptible by the senses and its accomplishment in ways appropriate to each of these signs. In it the full public worship is performed by the Mystical Body of Jesus Christ, that is, by the Head and his members.

"From this it follows that every liturgical celebration, because it is an action of Christ the Priest and of his Body, which is the Church, is a sacred action surpassing all others. No other action of the Church can equal its efficacy by the same title and to the same degree" (SC 7).

"From the liturgy, therefore, and especially from the Eucharist, grace is poured forth upon us as from a fountain, and the sanctification of men in Christ and the glorification of God to which all other activities of the Church are directed, as toward their end, are achieved with maximum effectiveness" (SC 10).

"In the restoration and promotion of the sacred liturgy the full and active participation by all the people is the aim to be considered before all else" (SC 14).

The communal nature of the liturgy is emphasized:

"It must be emphasized that rites which are meant to be celebrated in common, with the faithful present and actively participating, should as far as possible be celebrated in that way rather than by an individual and quasi-privately. This applies with special force to the celebration of Mass" (SC 27; see also SC 26).

"The rites should be distinguished by a noble simplicity. They should be short, clear, and free from useless repetitions. They should be within the people's powers of comprehension, and normally should not require much explanation" (SC 34).

"In sacred celebrations a more ample, more varied, and more suitable reading from Sacred Scripture should be restored" (SC 35).

"Provided that the substantial unity of the Roman rite is preserved, provision shall be made, when revising the liturgical books, for legitimate variations and adaptations to different groups, regions and peoples, especially in mission countries. This should be borne in mind when drawing up the rites and determining rubrics" (SC 38).

The second chapter of the Constitution on the Liturgy is especially concerned with the "most sacred mystery of the Eucharist."

"The Church, therefore, earnestly desires that Christ's faithful, when present at this mystery of faith, should not be there as strangers or silent spectators. On the contrary, through a good understanding of the rites and prayers they should take part in the sacred action, conscious of what they are doing, with devotion and full collaboration. They should be instructed by God's word, and be nourished at the table of the Lord's Body. They should give thanks to God. Offering the immaculate victim, not only through the hands of the priest but also together with him, they should learn to offer themselves" (*SC* 48).

To achieve this goal, Vatican II required a revision of the Order of Mass:

"The rite of the Mass is to be revised in such a way that the intrinsic nature and purpose of its several parts, as well as the connection between them, may be more clearly manifested, and that devout and active participation by the faithful may be more easily achieved.

"For this purpose the rites are to be simplified, due care being taken to preserve their substance. Parts which with the passage of time came to be duplicated, or were added with little advantage, are to be omitted. Other parts which suffered loss through accidents of history are to be restored to the vigor they had in the days of the holy Fathers, as may seem useful or necessary" (*SC* 50).

In accordance with these instructions, the Consilium for the Proper Implementation of the Constitution on the Sacred Liturgy reworked the section of the Missal containing those parts of the Mass that remain the same, the "Order of Mass." After some changes were made at the highest level, their work was approved and established as the rule through the apostolic constitution of Pope Paul VI, *Missale Romanum,*[9] issued on April 3 (Holy Thursday), 1969. A year later the complete Missal was published. It was preceded by the General Instruction of the Roman Missal (*GIRM*) and the General Norms for the Liturgical Year and the Calendar (*GNLYC*). In contrast to the earlier practice, the General Instruction not only contains rubrical instructions but also explains the content of the Mass.

[9] *DOL,* pp. 458–461.

Chapter Two

General Structure and Individual Parts of the Liturgy of the Mass

STRUCTURE OF THE WHOLE AND TABLE OF PARTS
Through the reform the basic framework of the celebration of the Mass has gained clarity and transparency:

"The Mass is made up as it were of the liturgy of the word and the liturgy of the eucharist, two parts so closely connected that they form but one single act of worship. For in the Mass the table of God's word and of Christ's body is laid for the people of God to receive from it instruction and food. There are also certain rites to open and conclude the celebration" (*GIRM* 8).

As we know, this structuring of the Mass in terms of two basic parts is already found in Justin Martyr, who wrote in the middle of the second century (see above, pp. 6–7).

There is no doubt that the statement of the General Instruction quoted above assigns greater value to the Liturgy of the Word, a part of the Mass that had previously usually been described as the "Foremass." Moral theologians considered that missing this part of the Mass was a "venial" sin, because it was only an insignificant part.[1] No wonder that so many people did not particularly worry about being on time for Mass.

[1] For example, this is the position of a handbook of moral theology that was widely used: Hieronymus Noldin, *Summa theologiae moralis*, 24th ed. (Innsbruck: Fel. Rauch, 1936) vol. 2, p. 243; Heribert Joné, *Moral Theology*, ed. and trans. Urban Adelman (Westminster, Md.: Newman Press, 1958): "*Venial sin* is committed by voluntarily omitting an unimportant part of the Mass, e.g., from the beginning of the Mass to the Offertory exclusive, or the part that follows the Communion, or even the part which precedes the Epistle together with that which follows the Communion" (p. 123).

TABLE OF INDIVIDUAL PARTS

General Structure	Meaning	Individual Part
1. Introductory rites	Uniting and preparing the congregation through penitence and prayer	Entrance song; veneration (kissing) of the altar; incensation of altar; sign of greeting and introduction; penitential rite; *Kyrie eleison*; *Gloria*; opening prayer
2. Liturgy of the Word	Proclamation of the word of God; meditation and response of the congregation	First reading and responsorial psalm. Second reading; acclamation before the gospel; (sequence); gospel and homily; Creed; intercessions
3. Eucharist (in narrower sense)	A. Preparation of the gifts; prayer of thanks over the bread and wine; act of offering one's self	Procession bringing gifts; prayers of preparation; incensation; washing of hands; prayer over the gifts
	B. Eucharistic Prayer; thanksgiving for God's saving acts; change of the bread and wine	Preface; *Sanctus*; epiclesis asking for the change of the gifts; institution narrative; acclamation; anamnesis; prayer of presentation; epiclesis asking for the fruits of Communion; intercessions; doxology
	C. Communion; union with Christ in the sacred meal	The Our Father; embolism; acclamation; rite of peace; breaking of bread; commingling; *Agnus Dei*; prayers of preparation; reception of Communion; giving thanks; concluding prayer
4. Concluding rite	Blessing and dismissal	Pastoral announcements; blessing; dismissal; kissing of altar and leaving

The table opposite outlining the general structure of the Mass applies especially to Eucharistic Prayers II and III. Special characteristics of Eucharistic Prayer I, commonly referred to as the Roman Canon, and of Eucharistic Prayer IV, which is a new creation related to the anaphoras of the Eastern liturgies, will be discussed later.

1. INTRODUCTORY RITES

Entrance Song

Even the first words of the rubrics provided at the beginning of the celebration of the Mass are essentially different from the corresponding instructions in the earlier (Tridentine) Missals. These older instructions speak only about the priest: how he is to prepare himself in the sacristy, which vestments he should put on, and his physical posture as he approaches the altar with "lowered eyes, reverential movements, and upright physical posture." In contrast to this, the first words of the new Missal dealing with the entrance are: "After the people have assembled, the entrance song begins as the priest and the ministers come in" (*GIRM* 25).

This already makes it clear that the assembled community is given a special value. Since this congregation is gathered in the name of Jesus, his promise applies to them: "Where two or three are gathered in my name, I am there among them" (Matt 18:20). This is the mysterious Body of Christ, the branch on the divine vine, the sanctified people of God, called to stand before and serve God.

One of the oldest documents that describe the celebration of the Eucharist is known as the *Teaching of the Twelve Apostles*, or the *Didache*. It views this Eucharistic gathering as a picture of the redeemed Church, which is symbolized by the many grains of wheat that have become one loaf of bread: "As this bread was scattered over the mountains and has now been brought back together, so will your Church be gathered from the ends of the earth into your kingdom" (chap. 9). This also explains why the ancient Church in the East called the Eucharistic celebration the *synaxis*, a Greek word meaning "gathering."

How different the many people are who come together to celebrate Mass! They come from the most varied conditions of life. Some are children, some youth, some adults, some aged; some are men, some are women. They come from the most varied social and vocational levels. Some come as poor, others as rich; some come with an air of joyous confidence, others depressed by disappointment and suffering. They come with their own personal characteristics and weaknesses, their own sharp corners and rough edges; perhaps they are also trapped in failure and guilt. And yet each participant in worship must recognize and affirm each of the others as a brother or sister, even when some "get on each other's nerves." No Christian may join the heathen poet Horace in saying, "I hate the common rabble and avoid them." God wills that each person should become a member of God's new people and has redeemed us all for this purpose. This is also true of the worshiping assembly, even though God's work in them is not yet finished. The liturgy of the Mass knows this well and therefore tries to use the introductory rites to prepare people's hearts for God's holy work.

In spite of its imperfections, this gathered community becomes a sign of, and a source of strength for, faith. In its common praying and singing it praises the triune God, who has given them salvation in Christ through the Holy Spirit. This community becomes a pilgrim fellowship of the redeemed. A poet has rightly described it as a gathering in which "each is both the staff and the burden of the other. They rest in common and walk in common toward their heavenly goal."[2]

The entrance of the priest and the other ministers admits of various stages of celebration. They should resist the temptation to take the shortest route from the sacristy (perhaps adjoining the chancel) but should rather choose to enter down the main aisle, assuming that the floor plan of the building makes that possible. This was the plan of the old Roman basilicas. In these buildings the sacristy was located next to the main entrance. The General

[2] "Der eine Stab des andern und süsse Last zugleich. Gemeinsam Rast und Wandern und Ziel das Himmelreich" (source unknown).

18

Instruction prescribes the following order for the procession (*GIRM* 82):

a. server with a lighted censer, if incense is used;
b. the servers, who, according to the occasion, carry lighted candles, and between them the cross bearer;
c. acolytes and other ministers;
d. a reader, who may carry the Book of the Gospels [if no deacon is present];
e. the priest who is to celebrate the Mass [concelebrants precede the priest; see *GIRM* 162].

If incense is used, the priest puts some into the censer before the procession begins (*GIRM* 82).

When the participants in the procession reach the altar, they bow deeply. If there is a tabernacle containing the Blessed Sacrament, they genuflect (*GIRM* 84). ''If the cross has been carried in the procession, it is placed near the altar or at some other convenient place; the candles carried by the servers are placed near the altar or on a side table; the Book of the Gospels is placed on the altar'' (*GIRM* 84).

The entrance is usually accompanied by a song. ''The purpose of this song is to open the celebration, intensify the unity of the gathered people, lead their thoughts to the mystery of the season or feast, and accompany the procession of priest and ministers'' (*GIRM* 25). The Missal provides the entrance antiphon. A solemn way of using this would be for the schola or the choir to sing this verse as the beginning and the end, the cantor singing an appropriate psalm and the congregation singing the accompanying response. A simpler form consists in the assembly singing a song corresponding to the festival or the liturgical season. Under no circumstances should the congregation be assigned the role of silent listeners.

Kissing of the Altar and Incensation
The priest (together with the concelebrants and the deacon) approaches the altar and kisses it. The Christian altar is a symbol of Christ; the crucified and risen Lord will be present on the holy

table, and from this table he communicates himself to the faithful as food and drink. For this reason, kissing the altar is a way of greeting and honoring Christ as the high priest and host of this feast. The priest carries out this greeting as the representative of the community, and the whole congregation should join inwardly in this act of greeting.

On feast days the priest may also incense the altar, that is, cover it with the smoke of the incense. Many people are not able to deal with such a ceremony, which has its beginnings long ago in the pre-Christian period. For this reason we shall make a few comments on the significance of incense, which is also used on other occasions in the Church's worship.

Incense is a mixture of the resins from various trees. We know that it was already used in the worship services of the Old Testament and by ancient heathens. At first Christians rejected its use, because the placing of incense before the statues of heathen gods was considered an act of sacrifice. In the Constantinian era, however, it began to be used in the East also in Christian worship. It was understood as a symbol of prayer, based on Psalm 141:2 ("Let my prayer be counted as incense before you"), and of self-consuming love of God and neighbor. It was also considered to be a sign of the Church's reverence and of its intercessory prayer. Thus, in addition to the altar, the Book of the Gospels, the crosses, and images, the ministers, and the assembly are also incensed. It would be a mistake to view the incense as a gift to God, as a material offering. However, anyone who understands its capacity to serve as many different symbols simultaneously will readily agree that incense is a "sermon without words."

A special form of incensing the altar has developed: The priest walks around the altar while incensing it, and particularly the cross on or behind the altar (see *GIRM* 236).

The Sign of the Cross
After kissing and incensing the altar, the priest takes his place at the presidential chair and leads the remaining introductory rites, the Liturgy of the Word, and the concluding rites from there. This

20

chair should be designed and located in such a way that it will make this leadership function clear. Under no circumstances should it resemble a throne (*GIRM* 271), for the ministers of the Church are not the rulers but the servants of the community.

Next the priest signs himself with the sign of the cross while saying, "In the name of the Father, and of the Son, and of the Holy Spirit." This contains a double confession: Our salvation is based only on the cross of Christ. "There is no other name under heaven given among mortals by which we must be saved" (Acts 4:12). Christ's redeeming death on the cross, however, is to become a sacramental presence in this celebration. The accompanying words are a confession of the triune God, the source and goal of our salvation.

At the same time, the sign of the cross made in the name of the triune God becomes a way of remembering our baptism. In his name we were born again in baptism and made members of the people of God. We have been plunged into the same paschal mystery of the Lord: "Do you not know that all of us who have been baptized into Christ Jesus were baptized into his death? Therefore we have been buried with him by baptism into death, so that, just as Christ was raised from the dead by the glory of the Father, so we too might walk in newness of life" (Rom 6:3-4). Because actions that are frequently repeated are in danger of losing beauty in their outward form as well as losing the power and depth that come from inner participation, the following statement by Romano Guardini deserves careful consideration:

"When we cross ourselves, let it be with a real sign of the cross. Instead of a small cramped gesture that gives no notion of its meaning, let us make a large, unhurried sign, from forehead to breast, from shoulder to shoulder, consciously feeling how it includes the whole of us, our thoughts, our attitudes, our body and soul, every part of us at once, how it consecrates and sanctifies us. It does so because it is the sign of the universe and the sign of our redemption. . . . It is the holiest of all signs."[3]

[3] Romano Guardini, *Sacred Signs*, trans. Grace Branham (St. Louis: Pio Decimo Press, 1956), pp. 13f.

Greeting and Introduction

After the sign of the cross, the priest greets the congregation. The General Instruction combines a high sense of purpose with this greeting: "Through his greeting the priest declares to the assembled community that the Lord is present. This greeting and the congregation's response express the mystery of the gathered Church" (*GIRM* 28). In defining this meaning, the Missal certainly does not intend to exclude a hearty personal tone from the greeting. After all, this assembly is made up of people whom the priest may possibly have not seen for some time. He may wish to take this opportunity, at the beginning of worship, to greet them and to affirm his personal relationship to them.

However, this greeting should not be spoken in a casual manner or maybe even embellished with various joking comments. There are more than a few participants in every service of worship who are full of sorrow, suffering, and grief and have come seeking comfort and power to bear their heavy fate. For this reason a definite reserve and objectivity are recommended.

The official greeting texts of the Missal provide this reserve and objectivity without requiring the elimination of a tone of heartfelt personal greeting. The Latin and English Missals provide three different forms of greeting for the priest to choose from; the German Missal provides eight. These are either texts of Sacred Scripture or are inspired by it, and are so formulated that the congregation can respond with the greeting "And also with you."

These greetings are spoken by the priest with extended hands, a symbolic action that can be understood in this context as an embrace. The greeting may be followed by a very brief introduction to the Mass. This introduction may be provided by a deacon or by someone else designated to provide it. Its purpose is to set the tone of a particular feast or to refer to the special character or intention of the Mass. In many cases the antiphon can be helpful in doing this. Ordinarily it is too early to provide an introduction to the readings from Scripture at this point. The introductory words should not be expanded into a first homily. The shorter, the better!

The Penitential Rite

The preparation rites should also include a rite of penance, that is, a repentant confession of guilt and a prayer for forgiveness. Whenever the Old Testament tells of encounters with God (theophanies), it describes the incidents as awakening consciousness of unworthiness and guilt. The persons encountered throw themselves to the ground and cover their face. Similarly in the New Testament, we frequently find this confession of unworthiness in the presence of the self-revealing God. No one who approaches the Holy Spirit should do so with feelings of pride or self-righteousness. Even the Christian needs to know how far he or she is removed from achieving the ideal: "If we say that we have no sin, we deceive ourselves, and the truth is not in us. If we confess our sins, he who is faithful and just will forgive us our sins and cleanse us from all unrighteousness" (1 John 1:8-9).

It is meaningful, indeed even necessary, for the faithful to be aware of their guilt at the very beginning of the Mass, to confess it, and to ask for forgiveness. In place of the former confession of sins (*Confiteor*) at the foot of the altar, the new Order of the Mass provides three forms of a penitential rite. They are introduced with an invitation to the faithful to confess their sins, followed by a brief pause for meditation, and conclude with a prayer for forgiveness spoken by the priest. The words of the invitation may also be formulated extemporaneously.[4]

The first form of the penitential rite consists of a common confession of sin that is based on the earlier *Confiteor*. We confess our guilt not only to "almighty God" but also to all our "brothers and sisters." This makes the social dimension of our failures clear. It consists not only in the fact that we, through our misdeeds, have done injustice to our fellow human beings and have violated love but also in the fact that we have injured the Body of Christ and destroyed what others are working to build up. Although this new *Confiteor* has been shortened, it has been essentially enriched through the addition of a confession of our having failed to do the good.

[4] *RM*, pp. 406–407.

More than a few Christians have difficulty in recognizing and confessing their guilt in the sacrament of reconciliation. One hears statements such as: "I don't know what to confess. I haven't stolen or murdered. I haven't committed adultery or perjury. I haven't even missed Mass on Sunday." The new *Confiteor* may be able to help us see that we can also become guilty by failing to do what is good. Not only have we failed to do works of mercy, but we have not been what the New Testament calls "the salt of the earth and the light of the world" and have not been available to our brothers and sisters as staff and support. There is a poem that says this very succinctly:

"Believe that they need you,
these people who walk through life with you;
they need your friendship and understanding,
your clear, sharp thinking,
which keeps itself free from rash judgment,
which knows faithfulness and speaks truth.
They need the purity of your character
and the clear power of your word,
and this is what they need most of all:
They need your knowledge of the eternal light."[5]

Measured by this demand, our life is a chain of failures to do the good, so that each of us can and must heartily participate in such a confession of guilt as incurred by us.

The *Confiteor* closes with the petition "I ask blessed Mary, ever virgin, all the angels and saints, and you, my brothers and sisters,

[5] Glaub nur, sie brauchen dich,
die Menschen, die mit dir gehen;
sie brauchen dein Gutsein und dein Verstehn,
dein blanken geraden Sinn,
der sich frei hält von raschem Gericht,
die Treue kennt und Wahrheit spricht.
Sie brauchen die Reinheit in deiner Gestalt
und deines Wortes klare Gewalt
und dies, was ihnen am meisten gebricht:
sie brauchen dein Wissen ums ewige Licht. (Maria Nels)

to pray for me to the Lord our God." This confession in one another's presence and the intercession for one another correspond to the instruction of the Letter of James (5:16): "Therefore confess your sins to one another, and pray for one another, so that you may be healed."

The second form of the penitential rite consists of a brief prayer prayed in alternation by the priest and the congregation. The third form combines three invocations of Christ together with the three acclamations of the *Kyrie* (to be discussed later). When this form is used, the *Kyrie* following the absolution is omitted.

In all the forms of the penitential rite the priest prays for forgiveness. This prayer should not be underestimated. "They are certainly not words of sacramental absolution for sins that require confession, but there can hardly be any doubt of their theological and sacramental significance for repentant sinners."[6]

The penitential rite may be completely omitted if the Mass is preceded by another liturgical act, such as some part of the Liturgy of the Hours, or in baptismal, wedding, and funeral Masses.[7] On Sundays the penitential rite may be replaced by the sprinkling of the congregation with holy water as a reminder of their baptism. This rite, which was very popular already in the earlier centuries, is described in the Sacramentary.[8] The priest begins by saying a prayer of blessing over the water, which "will be used to remind us of our baptism." Where customary, salt may be mixed into the water; the priest blesses the salt before pouring it into the water. He first sprinkles himself and the ministers with the water, and then the faithful. While this is taking place, an antiphon or an appropriate song is sung. One of these antiphons begins with the words *Asperges me* ("Cleanse me"), and as a result people sometimes speak of the "rite of aspersion." It concludes with a prayer

[6] Johannes H. Emminghaus, *The Eucharist: Essence, Form, Celebration,* trans. Matthew J. O'Connell (Collegeville, Minnesota: The Liturgical Press, 1978), pp. 119–120.

[7] See *RM,* p. 404, and Ralph A. Keifer, *To Give Thanks and Praise* (Washington: National Association of Pastoral Musicians, 1980), p. 115.

[8] *RM,* p. 404.

for cleansing from sin and sanctification through the sacrifice of the Mass being offered.

The Kyrie

The *Kyrie* follows (the Greek *Kyrie eleison* means "Lord, have mercy"). This is the remainder of an ancient intercessory litany of the kind that we now use at the end of the Liturgy of the Word. With the first word we pay homage to Christ, whom Paul frequently describes as the *Kyrios*, in the sense of the divine ruler. This phrase was used in heathen antiquity to pay homage to the gods or to a ruler who was revered as god. If we consider that Christians in the first centuries of the Christian era were often required to burn incense as an offering to the emperor as the *kyrios*, we can more easily understand that this acclamation became a conscious acknowledgment that Christ is the true *Kyrios*.

The second word, *eleison*, is a cry for divine mercy. As the blind and the lame, the lepers and sinners once called on the Lord to have mercy on them and the Lord responded by showing himself to be a helpful Lord, so we today, with our various physical and spiritual needs, trustfully call on Christ the Lord and ask him to be merciful. At the same time, we should also be fully aware that we as the Church must stand in solidarity with the poor and oppressed people of the whole world. In view of such millionfold needs and the endangered salvation of millions of people, we have every reason to describe the *Kyrie* acclamations as the Church's Advent prayer for the whole world.

The General Instruction emphasizes that the congregation ordinarily participates in the *Kyrie* acclamations (*GIRM* 30). Usually each acclamation (*Kyrie—Christe—Kyrie*) is sung twice. The insertion of short verses or tropes is permitted.

The Gloria

The General Instruction calls the *Gloria* "an ancient hymn in which the Church, assembled in the Holy Spirit, praises and entreats the Father and the Lamb" (*GIRM* 31). In the opinion of contemporary scholars, it is one of a group of early Christian hymns that "were composed in the style of the psalms and continue the tradition of the New Testament hymns."[9]

In the Byzantine Church the *Gloria* was used in the morning office (*Orthros*). It was first introduced into the Western Church as part of the celebration of Mass, usually only on especially solemn or festive occasions. It is now used "on Sundays outside Advent and Lent, on solemnities and feasts, and in special, more solemn celebrations (*GIRM* 31).[10]

As far as the structure of the *Gloria* is concerned, it is not difficult to determine that it contains three parts: the angels' song of praise, the glorification of God, and an act of praise and devotion to Christ.

Luke's description of the song of the angels above Bethlehem's fields (Luke 2:13f.) is the basic theme of the entire hymn. The original Greek text reads: "Glory is to God in the highest." This glorification of God is particularly apparent in the incarnation of his Son as the loving will of the triune God to give salvation. Jesus himself in his earthly life became the supreme example of the "glory of the Father"; we also confess that this is true in the doxology at the end of the Eucharistic Prayer. The fruit of this loving will to save is "peace to his people on earth." Here the word "peace" means what the Hebrew word *shalom* means: it includes all the gifts of salvation, comprehending all well-being of body and mind for the individual as well as complete harmony between people and God and among people themselves. Thus the angels' song of praise is a brief statement of the Good News in its entirety. The glorification of God that follows springs spontaneously from an amazed and thankful heart and rolls on like the waves of the ocean:

[9] Noelle Maurice Denis-Boulet, *Die Riten und Gebete der Messe,* in Aimé-Georges Martimort et al., eds., *Handbuch der Liturgiewissenschaft,* trans. Miriam Prager, ed. Liturgical Institute, Trier, vol. 1: *Allgemeine Einleitung. Die Grundelemente der Liturgie. Die Theologie der liturgischen Feier* (Freiburg: Herder, 1963), p. 358.

[10] See also Bishops' Committee on the Liturgy, *Music in Catholic Worship,* rev. ed. (Washington: United States Catholic Conference, 1983), p. 25.

"We worship you, we give you thanks,
we praise you for your glory."

The motivating theme of this overflowing adoration is once more
explicitly referred to as the "glory" of God. This makes it clear
that for Christians prayer is much more than petition. People who
turn to God only because they are up to their necks in trouble or
pray only for protection against evil are still standing on the porch
of Christian spirituality. For Christians, prayers of praise are both
existential realities that are taken for granted and their life's work.
The Church's liturgy of the canonical Hours ensures that these
prayers never cease; thereby the Church joins in the song of
praise which the incarnate Son of God brought with him to this
earth and which "is sung throughout all ages in the halls of
heaven" (SC 83).

At the end of this glorification the hymn once again refers to the
addressee of this adoration and reverently addresses him:

"For you alone are the Holy One,
you alone are the Lord,
you alone are the Most High."

These forms of address almost automatically make the transition
to the Lord Jesus Christ. As "God from God, Light from Light"
(Nicene Creed), he participates in the glory of the Father. In many
traditional texts of this hymn, the Holy Spirit is also named at this
point; often an "Amen" follows, making it clear that this verse of
the hymn has come to an end and a new one has begun.

This new verse expresses adoration of, and devotion to, Christ,
beginning with several majestic titles of the Redeemer: "Lord
(Kyrios) God, Lamb of God, Son of the Father." Each of these
titles is a brief statement of faith in Christ. Such trust in him leads
to a short litany of petitions:

"You take away the sin of the world:
    have mercy on us;
you are seated at the right hand of the Father:
    receive our prayer."

We can better understand the unique character of the closing glorification ("For you alone are the Holy One, you alone are the Lord, you alone are the Most High, Jesus Christ") if we keep in mind the period in which this hymn was created. It was the era of emperor worship, of splendid festivals of the gods, which included public sacrifices. These were followed by the persecution of Christians. Many laid claim to the title *Kyrios*. Anyone who refused to offer incense to them was under suspicion of being a threat to the public welfare, an enemy of God and of the state. This is the context that gave the confession of Christ its character as a life-and-death decision. Let no one think that this confession has lost this character in the contemporary situation. Even today false gods and seductive ideologies seek to impose themselves on people. Contemporary Christians are still required to confess in word and in life: "You alone are the Most High."

The hymn concludes with a confessional affirmation of the Trinity:

"Jesus Christ,
with the Holy Spirit,
in the glory of God the Father."

Anyone who sings or prays this ancient Christian hymn should be aware that true praise of the triune God does not end with the spoken word, but rather that the *Gloria* must be lived out in our lives. For this living out of the confession, however, there is no universal melody, no book of instructions that fits everyone's situation. The *Gloria* sounds different when it is sung in the fiery furnace of martyrdom than it does in the wearing attrition commonly experienced by people in the deadening routine of their everyday lives. Indeed, even the uncomplaining bearing of everyday burdens, illnesses, and psychological suffering, as well as helping others to bear their crosses, can all become a *Gloria* in praise of God. Every Mass on Sundays or festivals in which we participate summons us to renew this spirit of *Gloria Dei*.[11]

[11] In the early 1930's, Ludwig Wolker founded a German youth movement that was known as "Gloria Dei." Participation in this movement communicated insight and courage to many young people during the difficult times that began for Germany in the 1930's.

As far as the singing or reciting of the *Gloria* is concerned, we should observe the directive of the General Instruction: "It is sung by the congregation, or by the congregation alternately with the choir, or by the choir alone. If not sung, it is to be recited either by all together or in alternation" (*GIRM* 31). The German Missal allows the *Gloria* to be replaced by a song version of the *Gloria*. Unfortunately many of the songs chosen for this purpose do not do justice to the rich content of the hymn; although they praise God, they do not recapitulate the events of God's saving work in Christ.

The Opening Prayer or Collect

The introductory rites close with the "opening prayer," which is one of the presidential prayers among those to be prayed by the priest or bishop presiding over the celebration of the Eucharist. It is introduced by the invitation to prayer: "Let us pray." Although only the priest speaks the prayer, everyone who participates in the celebration becomes a pray-er of this prayer. This group of persons is also a unity, united in fellowship with Christ. For this reason the praying faithful are often referred to in this prayer as "your people," "your family," or "your Church." The Acts of the Apostles (4:32) describes the first congregation in Jerusalem as being "of one heart and soul." This remains the normative pattern for every Christian community.

After the invitation to pray, there is a brief period of silence. The General Instruction describes this: "They observe a brief silence so that they may realize they are in God's presence and may call their petitions to mind" (*GIRM* 32). Prayer and worship are not activities to be completed as quickly as possible. It is only in quietness that people can become aware of themselves and turn their hearts to God. In this silence individual worshipers are also able to clarify the identity of the persons and situations they are remembering in prayer.

The prayer that follows was formerly also called a "collect." This name was derived from the Latin term *oratio collecta*, which means "prayer that has been gathered and concentrated." It is deliberately brief so that all individual worshipers may include their individual prayers in it and know that they are included. The ancient Roman custom was to direct this prayer to the Father through the Mediator Jesus Christ in the Holy Spirit. Only since the tenth century have there been collects directly addressed to Christ. These were written under the influence of the Gaulish liturgy.

The content of these prayers consists of an address to God, followed by a relative clause that focuses on the theme of the celebration and by a petition. All opening prayers have a Trinitarian conclusion. The form of this conclusion depends on whether the petition is addressed to Father or the Son. The General Instruction prefers the first (more ancient) form: "The priest's words address a petition to God the Father through Christ in the Holy Spirit" (*GIRM* 32).

As is the case with all presidential prayers, the opening prayer is spoken with raised and extended hands. This is called the "stance of the *orantes*," the posture of the praying figures (*orantes*) depicted in the frescoes in the Roman catacombs. For early Christians, raising the arms and extending the hands during prayer was also a reminder of the posture of the crucified Lord. It is not only possible but very appropriate that this symbolic posture during prayer reminds Christians that Christ, during the celebration of the Mass, prays with them and for them as their High Priest.

In this context the custom of praying with folded hands should be discussed. At one time knights and feudal vassals placed their folded hands in the hands of their king or other feudal lord when they swore their oaths of fidelity or of feudal obligation. This symbolic action showed that they stood ready to serve their lord with heart and hands. It is not difficult to transfer the symbolic nature of this action to our stance before God. In addition, there is another posture of prayer in which we hold our clasped hands against our breast. This can be understood as a symbol of our inward focus and meditation. For this reason it is especially suited for use in private prayer.

The opening prayer ends when the people speak the Hebrew word *Amen*. This means, "Yes, it is so!" or "Yes, so be it!" With this word the congregation make the priest's prayer their own and simultaneously add their signatures to this document of prayer. Apparently the awareness of this was much more vital in the early Church than today. If this were not the case, how could the Church father St. Jerome report that the "Amen" spoken in the Roman basilicas reverberated through those spacious halls like heavenly thunder? This action still requires the active participation of the congregation. In fulfilling this role, they exercise the function assigned to them by the common priesthood of believers.

In contrast to the Order of Mass used before the Second Vatican Council, only one opening prayer is used. This is also the case with the prayer over the gifts and the prayer after Communion. According to the earlier order, it was possible to pray at least seven collects (including commemorations), and the sequence of these was prescribed down to the minutest detail.

The opening prayer used at weekday Masses in Ordinary Time may be chosen from several options: "On the weekdays in Ordinary Time, the prayers may be taken from the preceding Sunday, from another Sunday in Ordinary Time, or from the prayers for various needs and occasions listed in the Missal" (*GIRM* 323). The General Instruction sees this rich range of possibilities as creating "an opportunity continually to rephrase the themes of prayer for the liturgical assembly and also to adapt the prayer to the needs of the people, the Church, and the world" (*GIRM* 323).

2. THE LITURGY OF THE WORD
The Word of God in the Liturgy of the Mass
In this age of mass media, many voices and messages beat against our ears and seek admission. We are bombarded by audio and visual messages. We can avoid them only by listening with "half an ear," by letting many messages simply bounce off of us and by denying them admission to our minds.

One message, however, should always receive our special attention. This is the word that God has spoken to human beings, the word of the Sacred Scriptures. The Church is convinced that God uses these writings for self-revelation and wishes to use them to enlighten and empower us. The Second Vatican Council has proclaimed this truth as clearly and emphatically as possible:

"The Church has always venerated the divine Scriptures as she venerated the Body of the Lord, in so far as she never ceases, particularly in the sacred liturgy, to partake of the bread of life and to offer it to the faithful from the one table of the Word of God and the Body of Christ. She has always regarded, and continues to regard the Scriptures, taken together with sacred Tradition, as the supreme rule of her faith. For, since they are inspired by God and committed to writing once and for all time, they present God's own Word in an unalterable form, and they make the voice of the Holy Spirit sound again and again in the words of the prophets and apostles. . . . In the sacred books the Father who is in heaven comes lovingly to meet his children, and talks with them. And such is the force and power of the Word of God that it can serve the Church as her support and vigor, and the children of the Church as strength for the faith, food for the soul, and a pure and lasting fount of spiritual life" (DV 21).

The fathers of Vatican II symbolized the very great significance of the word of God in an especially impressive ceremonial: At the beginning of every session the Sacred Scriptures were carried in procession, accompanied by thurifers and acolytes, and were placed upon a throne, where they were honored with incensation.

Thus it is understandable that the Sacred Scriptures are also given a very important place in the liturgy of the Mass:

"For it is from [Scripture] that lessons are read and explained in the homily, and psalms are sung. It is from the Scriptures that the prayers, collects, and hymns draw their inspiration and their force, and that actions and signs derive their meaning" (SC 24).

Readings from Scripture are referred to already in the earliest post-apostolic description of the celebration of the Eucharist, the First Apology of Justin Martyr (chap. 67). Thus Vatican II was especially concerned to set the table of the word more lavishly and expand the opening to the treasure chest of the Bible (SC 51). The Council intended not only that larger quantities of Scripture should be read but also that these readings should be richer, more varied in content, and appropriate to the theme of the service.

Vatican II has sharpened our awareness that we are dealing with a mystery: God is working to achieve our salvation. That is exactly what St. Paul means in his First Letter to the Thessalonians: "We also constantly give thanks to God for this, that when you received the word of God that you heard from us, you accepted it not as a human word but as what it really is, God's word, which is also at work in you believers" (1 Thess 2:13). Twice Paul calls the word of God "the power of God" (Rom 1:16; 1 Cor 1:18). He also describes it as the word of life, of salvation, of grace, and of reconciliation.

Paul does not mean that this word tells us about these things but rather that it leads us to them and causes them to become realities. This word has divine creative power (see 1 Cor 4:15 and 1 Pet 1:23). Accordingly, the General Instruction of the Roman Missal says: "In the readings . . . God is speaking to his people, opening up to them the mystery of redemption and salvation, and nourishing their spirit; Christ is present to the faithful through his own word" (*GIRM* 33).

The word of God can reach and transform people at the deepest level of their being, but this is possible only through the power of the Holy Spirit. The introduction to the Lectionary for the Mass urgently emphasizes this:

"The working of the Holy Spirit is needed if the word of God is to make what we hear outwardly have its effect inwardly. Because of the Holy Spirit's inspiration and support, the word of God becomes the foundation of the liturgical celebration and the rule and support of all our life.

"The working of the Holy Spirit precedes, accompanies, and brings to completion the whole celebration of the liturgy. But the Spirit also brings home to each person individually everything that in the proclamation of the word of God is spoken for the good of the whole assembly of the faithful. In strengthening the unity of all, the Holy Spirit at the same time fosters a diversity of gifts and furthers their multiform operation" (*LMIn* 9).

This divine activity must be combined with attentive listening and openness to the biblical message.

In his parable of the sower and the seed, Christ himself warned against various mistaken attitudes in hearing the word of God. One exegete has summarized these inadequate forms of hearing in terms of three mistaken attitudes of the human heart: stupidity, thoughtlessness, and worldliness.[12]

An additional and very important perspective must be considered with respect to the Scripture readings in the liturgy. These readings must not be understood and explained only in terms of their historical meaning, for they are not intended only to inform us about past events; rather, they are God's message to people today. St. Augustine once put it this way: "We have learned about the previous event. Now we must find the hidden secret contained in this account."

To mention a few examples, the report of the miraculous multiplication of loaves has the primary purpose of telling us that this Jesus also is such a wonderful bread for us.[13] As such, he is the source of our strength. The gospel readings about healings and resurrections from the dead are intended to proclaim to us that we are the lepers, the blind, the lame, and the spiritually dead who experience these works of salvation from Jesus. Something corresponding to this is true also of the parables and addresses of Jesus, as well as for the letters of the apostles: We are the people who are addressed; we are the people who are spoken about and written about. As a result, the liturgical readings breathe the warm air of the present and tell us what is happening here and now or what it is that we have to do.

[12] Adolf Jülicher, *Die Gleichnisreden Jesu*, 2nd ed. (Tübingen: Mohr, 1910), vol. 2, p. 532.
[13] The words "miraculous" and "wonderful" in this sentence are used to translate the same German word: *wunderbar*. —*Trans.*

The New Order of Readings

The efforts to provide a richer selection of liturgical Bible readings resulted in the publication of the new *Ordo Lectionum Missae* (Order of Readings for Mass) on May 25, 1969. A second authorized edition, with an expanded pastoral introduction and the use of the Neo-Vulgate edition of the Bible, appeared on January 21, 1981. The most important provisions are the following:

Three readings are provided for all Sundays and solemnities. The first is from the Old Testament; the second is from the writings of the apostles; the third is from one of the Gospels. In order to expand the congregation's familiarity with the Sacred Scripture, a three-year series of readings has been introduced. These three series are designated by the letters A, B, and C. Series C is used in years that are divisible by three; the others follow in order.

The choice of readings was determined by two principles: appropriateness of their theme and the semicontinuous reading of a biblical book, that is, with some omissions. The first principle has determined the selection of the readings for the liturgically significant seasons of Christmas and Easter. On Sundays in Ordinary Time, the principle of semicontinuous reading of a book was determinative, that is, a biblical book is read section by section, except for omissions made for pastoral reasons. This continuous reading applies only to the second readings and to the gospels, whereas the Old Testament readings are selected to match the gospel of the day. In Year A, the Gospel of Matthew is read; in Year B, Mark; and in Year C, Luke. John's Gospel is used in the last weeks of Lent. The Acts of the Apostles is used for the first readings during the Easter season.

Many people had serious concerns about having three readings on Sundays and solemnities. A significant minority expressed their opposition at the Synod of Bishops held in Rome in 1967. The fear was that the greater quantity could have a detrimental effect on people inwardly. As a result, the Synod allowed each conference of bishops to decide whether two or three readings would be required.

The Order of Readings for weekdays generally proposes two biblical readings. There are two series of the first readings: Year I is used in uneven-numbered years, Year II in even-numbered years. The gospel readings, however, are the same in both years. These are so distributed that the Gospel of Mark is read in the first to ninth weeks of Ordinary Time, Matthew in the tenth to twenty-first weeks, and Luke in the twenty-second to thirty-fourth weeks. Special provisions appropriate to the character of the Christmas and Easter cycles have been made.

Additional orders of readings have been provided for the celebration of Mass on saints' days and for commemorations, for the celebration of the sacraments and sacramentals, for special occasions, and for votive Masses. All readings are to be read from a lectern called an "ambo"—the name is derived from the Greek word *anabainein*, meaning "to go up." The General Instruction of the Roman Missal says this about the significance of the ambo: "The dignity of the word of God requires the church to have a place that is suitable for proclamation of the word and is a natural focal point for the people during the liturgy of the word" (*GIRM* 272). It must fit into the space used for worship and be so placed that the reader can be easily seen and heard by all. The ambo is also used for the responsorial psalm, the gospel, and the Easter *Exsultet*; it may also be used for the homily and the prayer of the faithful (general intercessions).

According to tradition, the celebrant should not serve as the lector of the biblical readings if another reader is present. This makes it clear that the celebrating priest also places himself as a hearer under the word of God. While readings other than those from the Gospels can be read by a layperson, the gospel is always to be read by a deacon or priest.

First Reading and Responsorial Psalm
We have already stated that the first reading is taken from the Old Testament, except during the Easter season, when it is taken from the Acts of the Apostles, and that it has some correspondence to the gospel to be read in the Mass. By using Old Testament readings, the Church intends to make it clear that the Old Testament

is also divine revelation and that its ultimate purpose is to serve the saving events of Christ's life. According to a well-known statement of St. Augustine, the New Testament is hidden in the Old, and the Old Testament is revealed in the New. Vatican II's Dogmatic Constitution on Divine Revelation provides the following basic explanation:

"The economy of the Old Testament was deliberately so orientated that it should prepare for and declare in prophecy the coming of Christ, redeemer of all men, and of the messianic kingdom. . . . These books, even though they contain matters imperfect and provisional, nevertheless show us authentic divine teaching. Christians should accept with veneration these writings which give expression to a lively sense of God, which are a storehouse of sublime teaching on God and of sound wisdom on human life, as well as a wonderful treasury of prayers; in them, too, the mystery of our salvation is present in a hidden way" (DV 15).

The thematic correspondence of these readings to the gospel of the Mass may consist either in promise and fulfillment, in Old Testament parallels to the persons and events described in the gospel, or in thematic parallels, for example, the prophets' call to repentance and that of Jesus or his forerunner, or the calling of the prophets and that of the apostles, etc.

The congregation listens to the readings while seated. This relaxed body posture assists attentive listening. The lector concludes the readings with the acclamation "The word of the Lord," to which the congregation responds, "Thanks be to God."

It is possible to provide concise introductions to the readings. The introduction to the Lectionary for Mass requires that these introductions be carefully prepared: "They must be simple, faithful to the text, brief, well prepared, and properly varied to suit the text they introduce" (LMIn 15). Under no circumstances may they assume such a character that they anticipate the homily.

The first reading is followed by the responsorial psalm, which was previously also known as the "gradual." It has the function of marking the end of what has been heard and providing space for meditation. The General Instruction describes it as "an integral part of the liturgy of the word" (*GIRM* 36). The text is provided in the Lectionary and should ordinarily be sung. The introduction to the Lectionary for Mass describes two possibilities:

"There are two established ways of singing the psalm after the first reading: responsorially and directly. In responsorial singing, which, as far as possible, is to be given preference, the psalmist or cantor of the psalm sings the psalm verse and the whole congregation joins in by singing the response. In direct singing of the psalm there is no intervening response by the community; either the psalmist or cantor of the psalm sings the psalm alone as the community listens or else all sing it together" (*LMIn* 20).

"When not sung, the psalm after the reading is to be recited in a manner conducive to meditation on the word of God" (*LMIn* 22).

While the rubrics of the German Missal (335) provide that, when necessary, the responsorial psalm may be replaced by an appropriate song, the bishops of the United States have stated:

"Other psalms and refrains may also be used, including psalms arranged in responsorial form and metrical and similar versions of psalms, provided they are used in accordance with the principles of the *Simple Gradual* and are selected in harmony with the liturgical season, feast or occasion. The choice of the texts which are not from the psalter is not extended to the chants between the readings."[14]

Second Reading, Acclamation Before the Gospel, Sequence
The previous description of the new Order of Readings for Sundays and solemnities referred to the fact that the second reading is chosen on the basis of the principle that there should be some thematic correspondence to the mystery of the feast being celebrated. On Sundays of Ordinary Time, however, the principle of semicontinuous reading prevails. These readings are chosen from the letters of Paul and James. The letters of Peter and John

[14] *Music in Catholic Worship*, p. 24.

are read during the Christmas and Easter seasons. "Only readings that are short and readily grasped by the people have been chosen" (*LMIn* 107).

In spite of this, most of the faithful need some assistance in understanding the reading. This may be provided through a brief introduction to the reading and especially through the homily. One must accept the fact that it is not possible to explain everything in depth. Even with this limitation, people who regularly and attentively listen to the readings over the three-year cycle will become familiar with much of the Christian message. All that is needed is that as they listen they do what Luke says that the Mother of Jesus did: She kept these events in her heart and pondered them (see Luke 2:51).

The second reading is also concluded with the acclamation "The word of the Lord" and the response "Thanks be to God." The second reading is followed by the acclamation before the gospel. In contrast to the responsorial psalm, this acclamation is not a meditative response to a text that has been read but rather prepares for the gospel. It is an acclamation of Christ, who will be present in the gospel. Except during Lent, it consists of the Alleluia with its corresponding verse. *Alleluia* is a Hebrew word meaning "Praise Yahweh" and originated in Jewish worship. In all Christian liturgical rites, it is addressed to the risen Lord, corresponding to Revelation 19:1-7. Since it is such an Easter cry of homage, it is given a special place in the Easter season.

The verse that is framed by *Alleluias* is frequently taken from the following gospel reading. In accordance with the character of the Alleluia, it must be sung, and "is not to be sung only by the cantor who intones it or by the choir, but by the whole congregation together" (*LMIn* 23). During it all stand; this posture expresses the congregation's reverence for, and their readiness to receive, the One who is coming.

During the penitential season in preparation for Easter, the acclamation before the gospel consists of a greeting of welcome to Christ (for example, "Glory and praise to you, Lord Jesus Christ!")

40

and a verse. These are delivered in the same style as the Alleluia and its verse. The assertion of the introduction to the Lectionary that the Alleluia is a "rite or act standing by itself" (*LMIn* 23) applies to both forms of the acclamation before the gospel.

In addition to the two chants between the readings, another song has, since the early Middle Ages, found a place before the gospel. It is called a "sequence," a name derived from the late Latin term *sequentia*, meaning "continuation." This song developed as people began to add texts to the joyful melodies at the end of the Alleluia verses, melodies that were originally wordless. These texts were later expanded into symmetrical verses and rhymes. These sequences were popular in the Middle Ages. Some five thousand of these medieval sequences have been handed down. Since a fair number of these were, like weeds in a flower garden, not really suitable, the Missal of Pius V, published in 1570, limited the number of sequences to four.

The new post-Vatican II liturgy makes sequences obligatory on Easter and Pentecost (*GIRM* 40) and optional for Corpus Christi and Our Lady of Sorrows (September 15). The sequence is sung before the Alleluia because the Alleluia is the immediate preparation for the gospel.

The Gospel
The word "gospel," a word meaning "good news," is our brief designation for a selection from one of the four Gospels that is read in the Mass. It is the high point of the Liturgy of the Word. The introduction to the Lectionary for Mass puts it this way: "The reading of the gospel is the high point of the liturgy of the word. For this the other readings, in their established sequence from the Old to the New Testament, prepare the assembly" (*LMIn* 13).

Gerhard Ludwig Müller has pointedly asserted the special significance of the gospel in comparison with the other readings from the New Testament:

"The person who hears the gospel proclaimed does not merely encounter Jesus in a historical account or, as is the case in the New Testament epistles, in a confession to him or a reflection of his significance. Rather, the hearers of the gospel experience themselves as accompanying the earthly Jesus along the path of his life. They find that they are required to make decisions for or against the claims and demands that Jesus makes. Like the disciples, they are called to become followers of Jesus. As they accompany Jesus as he carries his cross to Golgotha in order to sacrifice his life to the Father, they are tested in their own life and suffering. They experience his resurrection and announce that all of us have a valid hope to live in eternal fellowship with God."[15]

This special character of the gospels makes it understandable that the gospel of the Mass is surrounded with festive ceremonies, as is also the custom in the Eastern Church. Among these signs of honor are:

a) The reader must be a priest or a deacon.

b) If he is a priest, he speaks the preparatory prayer: "Almighty God, cleanse my heart and my lips that I may worthily proclaim your gospel" (see Isa 6:6f.). If the reader is a deacon, he requests a blessing from the presiding priest. This blessing is: "The Lord be in your heart and on your lips that you may worthily proclaim his gospel."

c) The Book of the Gospels is carried in the entrance procession accompanied by servers with candles and incense and is placed on the lectern.

d) After the brief dialogue "The Lord be with you . . ." and the announcement of the name of the Gospel from which the reading is taken, the priest or deacon makes the sign of the cross on himself and on the book. In making the sign of the cross on himself, he makes a small sign of the cross on his forehead, mouth, and breast. The faithful are invited to make the same threefold cross on themselves. The origin of this custom is older than that of the usual sign of the cross. The meaning of this threefold sign of the cross before the gospel is read—a custom that has been observed in the West for over a thousand years—must be understood as a prayer for a blessing. John Beleth, a twelfth-

[15] Gerhard Ludwig Müller, *Lasst uns mit ihm gehen. Eucharistiefeier als Weggemeinschaft* (Freiburg: Herder, 1990), p. 68.

century theologian, sees it as expressing both the admonition and the readiness to stand up for the word of God unashamedly, without hiding our face, to confess it with our mouth, and to keep it faithfully in our hearts. The Book of the Gospels also receives the sign of the cross because it contains the message that the cross is the source of all blessing.

e) The priest or deacon incenses the book as a sign of honoring Christ who is present.

f) The faithful speak or sing special acclamations honoring Christ, such as "Glory to you, Lord" and "Praise to you, Lord Jesus Christ."

g) The congregation sits for the readings but stands to hear the gospel. This expresses their joy, reverence, and alertness. In this sense, their standing becomes a confession without words.

h) After the reading the priest or deacon kisses the book and prays: "May the words of the Gospel wipe away our sins." This liturgical act announces the saving power of the word of God.

This special reverence for the gospel both in the Eastern and Western Churches led to the preparation of a special book containing only the gospel readings used in the Mass. This book was always printed, bound, and illustrated with great artistry. The introduction to the Lectionary for the Mass recommends that this usage be reintroduced (*LMIn* 36).

"Where there is a Book of the Gospels that has been carried in by the deacon or reader during the entrance procession [and placed on the altar] . . ." (*LMIn* 17).[16] This instruction also expresses special honor and reverence for the gospel. This entrance procession with the Book of the Gospels follows the pattern of the liturgy of the Byzantine Rite, although the ceremonies of that rite are much richer.

The Homily (Sermon)
The homily interprets the passages of Sacred Scripture and the texts used in the common and proper sections of the Mass. Historically it is one of the earliest elements of the Liturgy of the

[16] Words in brackets are not in English text.

Word. Originally the homily was a special privilege of the bishop; today, however, it is normally given by the priest presiding at the celebration or even by the deacon.

In view of the fact that the homily during Mass was definitely neglected at some times and in some places, Vatican II emphasized that it is a part of the liturgy and may not be omitted, especially in the congregational Masses on Sundays and holydays of obligation (*SC* 52). The homily "is necessary for the nurturing of the Christian life" (*GIRM* 41). It is intended to let the word of God be heard in the words of human beings, to translate it in a convincing way into language that the hearers can understand, to demonstrate its power to clarify contemporary problems, and to make its summons to, and its claim on, the hearer understandable. In order to clarify the unity of the Liturgy of the Word and Liturgy of the Eucharist, it must both build the bridge between the story being celebrated and the paschal mystery, and at the same time make the hearer conscious of this saving event.

This demanding task differentiates the homily of the Mass from every secular address. The homily is "God's word in the mouth of a human being," and as such it participates, even though some steps removed, in the saving power of God's word. It compels people to the obedience of faith, to encountering Christ in the sacrament, and to living Christian lives. In this sense we can apply to the homily what Paul wrote to the Corinthians: "In Christ Jesus I became your father through the gospel" (1 Cor 4:15). It is a saving event in which Christ actively works the salvation of the hearer.

As far as the content and form of the homily are concerned, there are various possibilities:

a) *The homily as a preparatory word*
Not all participants in the service come with an appropriate disposition. Absent-mindedness, inability to concentrate, and deficiencies of faith, hope, and love make the approach to divine revelation and the sacramental mystery more difficult for some. The homily of the Mass must assist such people to develop inner still-

ness and concentration, to strengthen faith, to loosen the cramps of egoism, to remove bitterness and hate, and to make room for the encounter with Christ and loving affirmation of one's fellow human beings.

b) *The homily as an explanation of Sacred Scripture*
The biblical readings of the Mass do not merely contain a general report of the good news, but they also describe the particular mystery being celebrated in the solemnities and festive seasons. The homily of the Mass has the task of making this message understandable to its hearers and of showing them what it means for their lives. As the homily of the Mass, it may not ignore the original meaning of the readings but must make that meaning transparent to the contemporary saving work of Christ. In this way the homily acquires "the hot breath of our experience in the here and now, the burning vitality of the amazed soul" (S. Grün).

c) *The homily as an explanation of the Mass*
The second group of themes of the homily that the post-Vatican II documents refer to is the exposition of a text "from the Ordinary or from the Proper of the Mass of the day" (*GIRM* 41). The symbols and the symbolic actions associated with the Mass also contain specific statements and may therefore also be included in this group of theses. Experience indicates that many people who go to Mass, whether regularly or not, are largely ignorant of the broad array of symbolic actions present in the Mass.

d) *The homily as mystagogy*
There is a high form of the homily of the Mass that we may properly describe as mystagogy. The original meaning of "mystagogy" was the accompaniment of the initiates into an inner understanding and experience of the mysteries so that their daily lives would be shaped by them. In the ancient Church, mystagogy was a highly revered process and was practiced by persons such as Ambrose, Augustine, Zeno of Verona, Cyril and John of Jerusalem, and many others. It was rediscovered and promoted by the liturgical movement of the twentieth century.[17]

[17] See below, p. 109.

Mystagogical homilies of the Mass grow out of the Eucharistic liturgy and lead us into deeper participation in this liturgy. They assist us to join in the action of the Mass at a feeling level; they make us aware of the contemporary relevance of the paschal mystery as a "here and now" reality; they establish our solidarity with the Lord who gave himself for us and compel us to offer ourselves to the Father in heaven and in service of our fellow human beings. They give vitality to our thankful praise and demonstrate that our whole life must be a Eucharist. This does not happen because the homily is scholarly and rhetorically correct; rather, it depends on the immediate faithful experience of the mystery, on experiencing its presence on an emotional level. To this extent, a mystagogical homily will be quite different from one that is merely based on liturgical scholarship or that provides dogmatic instruction.

e) *The homily addresses problems of contemporary life*
In addition to the groups of themes already mentioned, the post-Vatican II documents (for one example among many, see *GIRM* 41) require that the homilies "take into account . . . the needs proper to the listeners." This certainly means that the homily of the Mass must also take into account the many ways in which the listeners' experience threatens their faith, in which their understanding of themselves as Christians is being battered, and the special problems they confront at this time and in this place.

It is simply not possible to assume that the Mass has no responsibility to respond to these tasks because these tasks will be met by non-Eucharistic services or other parish activities. In fact, the Sunday Eucharistic service is the only possibility available to most of the faithful to gain a clear understanding of the meaning of their faith for the questions that confront them in life. It should be taken for granted that a homily that is relevant to contemporary needs must also be God- and Christ-centered. Such homilies move in concentric orbits around these centers; like the planets orbiting the sun, they may be at different distances from the center but are all held in place by the same forces.

In closing, it may be asserted that the homily of the Mass is one of the most important and effective pastoral efforts of the present. It is not some amusement center in which we may follow any flight of fancy, but rather it makes significant demands on the preacher. The listeners also play their part in contributing to the success of the homily of the Mass, as has already been noted.

The homily should conclude with a brief period of meditation. This is also an integral element of the celebration (*GIRM* 23).

The Profession of Faith (Creed)
The biblical readings and the homily have made us hear God's word. Now the congregation is summoned to respond to them with a clear "yes" expressed both in their profession of faith and in their faithful lives. They do this explicitly in their common confession of faith. It is an extended "Amen" to the liturgy of the Word. According to the new Order of Mass, all join in speaking (or singing) this on all Sundays and solemnities. In addition, it may also be said at "special, more solemn celebrations" (*GIRM* 44).

The Creed appeared in the celebration of the Mass at a relatively late date. It appeared first in the Eastern liturgies at the beginning of the sixth century and then in Spain at the end of the sixth century. It did not become part of the Roman liturgy until early in the eleventh century. The Creed that was used was that of the "great" profession of faith, the creedal symbol adopted by the Council of Nicaea in 325 and revised by the Council of Constantinople in 381 (the Nicene-Constantinopolitan Creed). This Creed was based on the profession of faith used in the East at baptismal services, whereas the Western Church used the Apostles' Creed for this purpose.

The meaning of the Creed in the context of the celebration of the Mass becomes apparent only when viewed from several perspectives:

a) Viewed as the original profession of faith at our baptism, it reminds us of our baptism and thereby summons the congregation to renew their baptism. At the same time, this documents the close relationship between baptism and Eucharist. These two sacraments, together with confirmation, constitute the sacraments by which we become members of the Body of Christ. They are the so-called sacraments of initiation.

b) We live in a time in which public opinion and "common sense" generally know and recognize only those realities and standards that are derived from our experience of the world. In such a time people establish themselves as the highest authorities and the measure of all things, so that Christ's saving work, his promises of salvation and directions on how to find it, all threaten to be forgotten. For this reason we especially need to frequently encounter statements of the content of our faith that require us to renew our decision to believe. That is what happens when we speak the Creed while celebrating the Mass. Here the congregation experiences itself over and over as the fellowship of the faithful, as the Church that professes its faith in Christ and bears witness to him.

In addition, the individual members of the assembly should speak this profession of faith in the awareness that they thereby become part of the procession of witnesses to the faith and martyrs of the past and the present, whose number is beyond counting. Such a consciousness makes us more loyal believers and gives us courage to make our personal confession of faith.

c) As part of the liturgy of the Mass, the Creed also praises the God who works our salvation. Without using words that explicitly praise and glorify God, it is like a hymn proclaiming the great acts of the triune God. In this way it is related both to the *Gloria* and to the Eucharistic Prayer, especially to the preface of that prayer. Since the Apostles' Creed is rooted in the liturgy of baptism of the Western Church, it may be used in Masses with children.

The Creed may be recited or sung (*GIRM* 44). All stand during the profession of faith (*GIRM* 21).

One special instruction that applies when the profession of faith is spoken or sung still needs to be mentioned. When the Creed speaks of Christ becoming man and of his birth, all bow, but on the feasts of Christmas and Annunciation all kneel (*GIRM* 98). This is a gesture of reverence in response to the incomprehensible way in which God has condescended to begin the redemptive work of Christ. At this point we do just what the wise men from the East did when they saw the child and his mother: "They knelt down and paid him homage" (Matt 2:11.).

The Petitions (Prayer of the Faithful)
The Liturgy of the Word concludes with the petitions, also called the "prayer of the faithful" or the "general intercessions." They are one of the elements of the liturgy that the Constitution on the Sacred Liturgy refers to when it says: "Other parts which suffered loss through accidents of history are to be restored to the vigor they had in the days of the holy Fathers" (SC 50). These intercessions had been lost to the rite of the Mass for almost fifteen hundred years. They were preserved only in the solemn orations used on Good Friday and in their remaining traces in the *Kyrie*. Now the people of God once again make intercession for all of humanity, for all needs and dangers in the Church and in the world. The General Instruction of the Roman Missal describes this prayer as follows:

"In the general intercessions or prayer of the faithful, the people, exercising their priestly function, intercede for all humanity. It is appropriate that this prayer be included in all Masses celebrated with a congregation, so that petitions will be offered for the Church, for civil authorities, for those oppressed by various needs, for all people, and for the salvation of the world" (*GIRM* 45).

Such intercession breaks through the narrow horizon of ego-centricity and awakens responsibility for the great concerns of humanity and the whole Church. In so doing, the congregation explicitly participates in the common priesthood received in baptism and confirmation. The assembly takes its place by the side of its Lord, "who gave himself a ransom for all" (1 Tim 2: 6), whose life and work consisted of being there for others. With him and in him, the gathered community intercedes for all of humanity and thereby realizes the admonition of the First Letter of Timothy:

"First of all, then, I urge that supplications, prayers, intercessions, and thanksgivings be made for everyone, for kings and all who are in high positions, so that we may lead a quiet and peaceable life in all godliness and dignity. This is right and is acceptable in the sight of God our Savior, who desires everyone to be saved and to come to the knowledge of the truth (1 Tim 2:14)."

The Christian faith understands such prayer for others to be especially effective when it is spoken as a prayer of the community, because Christ is then united to, and in solidarity with, those praying, according to Matthew 18:19-20: "Again, truly I tell you, if two of you agree on earth about anything you ask, it will be done for you by my Father in heaven. For where two or three are gathered in my name, I am there among them."

The official guidelines for the formulation of intercessions provide that the priest speak the introductory invitation to prayer and the concluding prayer. The intentions of the prayers should normally be announced by the deacon, the cantor, or one or more members of the congregation. The assembly itself accompanies these petitions with responses or silent prayer. In the latter case, enough time must be provided for such silent prayer. As a rule, the sequence of the intentions is to be: (a) for the needs of the Church; (b) for public authorities and the salvation of the world; (c) for those oppressed by any need; (d) for the local community. In particular celebrations, such as confirmations, marriages, funerals, etc., the series of intercessions may refer more specifically to the occasion (*GIRM* 46). This especially means that in these cases more intentions may be offered for those who are present.

Theodor Schnitzler has protested against a misformation of the intercessions:

"The intercessions are not short sermons, not brief creeds, not editorials from the daily newspaper, not media commentaries, and absolutely never contributions to current political discussions. Sometimes organizations, institutions, or the administrative offices of associations distribute texts of intercessions proposed for use in worship. Often such proposed intercessions kindly instruct

Heaven about what is happening here and what God needs to do to help. In the process, both heavenly and earthly listeners are once again clearly reminded of the organization's own agenda."[18]

3. THE LITURGY OF THE EUCHARIST

Following the Liturgy of the Word, the first main part of the celebration of the Mass, the second main part, the Liturgy of the Eucharist (in the narrow sense of the term) begins. Its structure was prefigured in the Last Supper of Jesus, as the General Instruction explicitly emphasizes:

"Christ took the bread and the cup and gave thanks; he broke the bread and gave it to his disciples, saying: 'Take and eat, this is my body.' Giving the cup, he said, 'Take and drink, this is the cup of my blood. Do this in memory of me.' Accordingly, the Church has planned the celebration of the eucharistic liturgy around the parts corresponding to these words and actions of Christ:

1. In the preparation of the gifts, the bread and the wine with water are brought to the altar, that is, the same elements that Christ used.

2. In the eucharistic prayer thanks is given to God for the whole work of salvation and the gifts of bread and wine become the body and blood of Christ.

3. Through the breaking of the one bread the unity of the faithful is expressed and through communion they receive the Lord's body and blood in the same way the apostles received them from Christ's own hands" (*GIRM* 48).

A. THE PREPARATION OF THE GIFTS

Older people will still remember that, before the reform of the Order of the Mass, the first part of the Liturgy of the Eucharist was called the "offertory." This expression could easily lead to misunderstandings. The "presentation" (Latin: *offerre*, "to bring, present, offer") of bread and wine was originally a simple process

[18] Theodor Schnitzler, *Was die Messe bedeutet*, 11th ed. (Freiburg: Herder, 1990), p. 112.

of preparation, that is, of bringing these gifts that were to be changed. Gradually the faithful included contributions for the support of the clergy, the poor, and also the church building. In many parts of the Church this became a procession bringing the gifts and was known as the "offertory procession."

In New Testament worship such gifts could be referred to as "sacrifices" only in an improper sense. For since Christ died on the cross, the Old Testament offerings of animals, food, and incense have become antiquated and cease to exist. In spite of this, in the early Middle Ages, especially in the areas where the Gaulish-Frankish liturgies were practiced, these gifts were considered almost cultic sacrifices. In many parts of the Church the procession with the gifts was also called a sacrificial procession or an offertory procession.

This led to the development of many prayers and ceremonies, some of which also were incorporated into the Roman liturgy of the Mass. These could give the impression that we were already at this point in the Mass dealing with the transformed gifts. Thus, until the reform of the liturgy after Vatican II, the priest, while elevating the bread, said: "Accept, O holy Father, almighty and eternal God, this spotless host which I, your unworthy servant, offer to you, my living and true God . . . on behalf of all here present . . . that it may profit me and them as a means of salvation to life everlasting." While elevating the chalice, he said: "We offer you, O Lord, the chalice of salvation. . . ." This was soon followed by an epiclesis offered over the gifts ("Come, O Sanctifier . . . and bless this sacrifice . . ."). After washing his hands, he began the prayer to the Blessed Trinity: "Accept, most holy Trinity, this offering which we are making to you. . . ."[19]

It is too early in the Mass to use such formulations, and they were therefore misplaced. The best way of interpreting them is to say that these thoughts anticipate the later changing of the elements and the sacrificial act involving these gifts—something that hap-

[19] The translations of the prayers in this paragraph are taken from *Saint Joseph Daily Missal*, rev. ed., ed. Hugo H. Hoever (Kansas City, Mo.: I. Donnelly Co., 1959), pp. 659–665.

pens only in the context of the Eucharistic Prayer. Unfortunately the new Missal contains a text that is subject to a similar misinterpretation:

"Pray, brethren, that our sacrifice
may be acceptable to God, the almighty Father."

It was completely right, therefore, to replace the word "offertory" (Latin: *offertorium*) with the term "preparation of the gifts" (Latin: *praeparatio donorum*); the latter term accurately describes what is happening. In addition, it parallels the corresponding Greek term (*proskomide*) in the Byzantine liturgy. Having clarified these basic matters, we turn our attention to the individual elements of the preparation of the gifts.

Preparing the Altar

At the beginning of the preparation of the gifts, the altar, which is the place at the center of the Eucharistic liturgy, is prepared to serve as the "table of the Lord" (1 Cor 10:21). Its special dignity derives primarily from the fact that through the Eucharistic mystery it becomes the "throne of Christ." The altar was already highly regarded and honored in the first Christian centuries. Its holiness, therefore, does not come from the tabernacle, which was first placed on the altar in the sixteenth century. It is "the table of the Lord and the people of God are called together to share in it. The altar is, as well, the center of the thanksgiving that the eucharist accomplishes" (*GIRM* 259).

Some of the new ecclesiastical instructions are especially noteworthy: The altar "should be freestanding to allow the ministers to walk around it easily and Mass to be celebrated facing the people. It should be so placed as to be a focal point on which the attention of the whole congregation centers naturally" (*GIRM* 262). As a sign of reverence for the holy meal, the altar should be covered with at least one cloth. "The shape, size, and decoration of the altar cloth should be in keeping with the design of the altar" (*GIRM* 268). "Candles are . . . a sign of reverence and festiveness" of the various liturgical rites. "The candlesticks are to be placed either on or around the altar" (*GIRM* 269). "There is also to be a cross, clearly visible to the congregation, either on the altar or near it" (*GIRM* 270). The cross is a clear sign of the fact that Christ's sacrifice on the cross is re-presented in the celebration of the Mass.

The new Rite of Dedication of a Church and an Altar,[20] which appeared in 1977, forbids the placing of statues, pictures, or relics of saints on the altar of new churches. It is the nature of the altar that it is dedicated to the one God, because the Eucharistic sacrifice is presented to this one God, even though it may be combined with the veneration of certain saints (chap. IV, 10).

The custom of decorating the altar with flowers is mentioned in an official liturgical document for the first time in this rite for the dedication of an altar (chap. IV, 10 and 27; *Rites*, pp. 414 and 427). Given the analogy of decorative flowers at a festive meal, there is certainly no reason to object to the custom, as long as the flowers do not block the free view of what is happening at the altar.

The preparation of the altar that takes place at the beginning of the preparation of the gifts consists in bringing the corporal, purificator, missal, and chalice to the altar (*GIRM* 49). (The corporal is a square linen cloth on which the chalice and the dish containing the hosts are placed; the purificator is a small cloth for cleansing the chalice.)

Previously it was customary to place the corporal on the altar before the celebration of the Mass began and to place the chalice covered with a veil on the corporal. It is hoped that the new directions will result in more clearly identifying the beginning of the celebration of the Eucharist, in the narrow sense, since "the holy table" is prepared only after the Liturgy of the Word has ended. Of course, one could argue that at a festive banquet the table is also set before the guests arrive, even if the meal is preceded by festive addresses. Thus there are many reasons for preserving the earlier order, especially since the beginning of the

[20] The ICEL translation of "Dedication of a Church and an Altar," in *Rites*, vol. 2, pp. 341–448, was published in 1982. *DOL*, pp. 1370ff., contains the introductions to the various rites.

preparation of the gifts is visibly symbolized by the fact that this is the first time during the service that the priest approaches the altar.

The Procession with the Gifts

The preparation of the bread and wine was not a ritual act originally. The bringing of these gifts acquired a certain festiveness only gradually: The faithful began to bring bread and wine and charitable gifts in procession to the altar rail, handing them over to the deacon or priest. Augustine already informs us that in the larger churches this procession was accompanied by a psalm. In Rome this song during the procession with the gifts was called the *antiphona ad offertorium* ("offertory antiphon"). At the time of Charlemagne, the gifts and the altar began to be incensed.

The new Missal states:

"It is desirable for the faithful to present the bread and wine, which are accepted by the priest or deacon at a convenient place. The gifts are placed on the altar. . . . Even though the faithful no longer, as in the past, bring the bread and wine for the liturgy from their homes, the rite of carrying up the gifts retains the same spiritual value and meaning" (*GIRM* 49).

This spiritual meaning consists in the fact that the faithful intend to offer themselves together with their gifts in the Eucharistic celebration. Their faith and inner surrender of themselves is in harmony with the self-giving of the Lord, who sacrifices himself for us. This self-offering of the Church will be treated in more detail when we discuss the Eucharistic Prayer.

This inner devotion is also symbolized if, in addition to bread and wine, charitable gifts are brought, such as the usual collections. These material contributions are really an expression of helping love, which Christ refers to himself ("Just as you did it to one of the least of these who are members of my family, you did it to me"—Matt 25:40), and of responsibility for the world and the Church. When understood in this way, the regular collections of money in the service of worship lose the tone of burdensome begging and become part of the preparation of the gifts. Care should be taken to complete these collections before the beginning of the preface; this can easily be achieved by having several persons gathering the collection or by using several baskets.

The baskets used in the collections and other contributions are "to be put in a suitable place but not on the altar" (*GIRM* 49). If this place is close to the altar, the spiritual relation of these gifts to the celebration of the Mass will be made especially clear.

"The procession can be accompanied by a song. Song is not always necessary or desirable. Organ or instrumental music is also fitting at this time. . . . If there is no singing or organ or instrumental music, this may be a period of silence" (*GIRM*, Appendix, no. 50). Songs and hymns appropriate to the preparation of the gifts or to the liturgical season or the particular feast day may be used. The German Missal recommends the Latin offertories of the *Ordo Cantus Missae* or of the *Roman Gradual* and the *Simple Gradual* as appropriate songs. However, one should also remember the possibility that the preparation of the gifts may be a period of quiet, especially since the preceding Liturgy of the Word and the following Eucharistic Prayer are not appropriate times for extended silence.

The Prayer of Thanksgiving over the Bread and Wine
Vatican II had given instruction that the Order of the Mass be revised in a way "that will bring out more clearly the intrinsic nature and purpose of its several parts, as also the connection between them, and will more readily achieve the devout, active participation of the faithful" (*SC* 50). The members of the study group working on the reform of the Mass thought it necessary to replace the prayers of preparation previously used with better prayers. Numerous formulations were considered in this process. Finally they agreed on a text that is modeled after the Jewish prayers of thanksgiving (*berakoth*). This prayer is spoken when the bread and the wine are lifted up from the altar:

"Blessed are you, Lord, God of all creation.
Through your goodness we have this bread (wine) to offer, which earth has given and human hands have made.

It will become for us the bread of life (*for the wine:* our spiritual
  drink).
℟. Blessed be God for ever."

The rubrics of the Mass instruct the priest to speak these texts
inaudibly. However, if there is neither singing nor organ music
at this time, he may speak them audibly.

Both prayers of preparation begin with praise of the Creator.
Bread and wine are described as God's gifts. The statement of the
Letter of James (1:17) applies here: "Every generous act of giving,
with every perfect gift, is from above, coming down from the
Father of lights."

For many millennia bread has been the basic nourishment of
many peoples. It makes life possible. The English word "victuals"
is ultimately derived from the Latin word *vivere,* meaning "to
live." Without such nourishment, people will die. Thus the gift of
bread reminds us of God as the creator, preserver, and friend of
life. The same is true of the wine, which ancient Israel considered
to be a means of nourishment and of salvation, as well as a means
of enjoyment.

Anyone who considers that we receive our nourishment as a gift
will thank God, that is, will pray. The prayer over the meal is an
ancient human custom that is still meaningful today. Prayer gives
every meal a religious component, making it a kind of dedication.
Such prayer creates fellowship and friendship, peace and joy.
Thus Christ could use bread and wine as a visible symbol of that
meal in which he himself becomes our food, in which he gives us
fellowship with one another and with the triune God, and which
is a pledge of the eternal marriage feast.

The prayers of preparation refer not only to the Creator but also
to the people whose difficult labors have planted the grain and the
vines, harvested and processed their fruits, so that they have become nourishment for us. Bread and wine involve so much labor
that we might call them a piece of human existence; they are
fruits of human work. They also become symbols of the human
beings themselves who bring these gifts as an offering to Christ.

The earliest Christian tradition (for example, the *Didache*) viewed the bread and wine, made up of many grains of wheat and many grapes and given a new form, as a symbol of the unity in which those who receive these transformed gifts are themselves transformed into the community of Christ, indeed even grow together into his Body. This symbolism will be discussed in more detail later when we deal with Communion.

As far as the actual nature of the bread and wine is concerned, the bread must be prepared according to the provisions of the General Instruction: "The bread must be made only from wheat and must have been baked recently; according to the long-standing tradition of the Latin Church, it must be unleavened" (*GIRM* 282).

This custom of using unleavened bread developed in the West only during the period from the ninth to the eleventh century. The Byzantine Church, which uses leavened bread, took serious offense at this. At the Council of Florence in 1439, both sides agreed that the body of Christ is present both in unleavened and in leavened bread; however, each priest must conform to the rites of his own Church. Over the centuries the custom grew of baking increasingly thinner wafers that were more and more white. These wafers were imprinted with religious symbols using an iron implement. All this has unfortunately led to a significant loss of the symbolic power of these hosts, since people can hardly recognize that they are still bread.

For this reason the new Missal requires that "the material for the Eucharistic celebration truly have the appearance of food." The hosts should also be made "in such a way that in a Mass with a congregation the priest is able actually to break the host into parts and distribute them to at least some of the faithful. When, however, the number of communicants is large or other pastoral needs require it, small hosts are in no way ruled out" (*GIRM* 283).

It is required that the wine "be from the fruit of the vine (see Luke 22:18), natural, and pure, that is not mixed with any foreign substance" (*GIRM* 284). Although the Eastern Churches prefer red wine, the Western Church has used white wine since the six-teenth century. The reason for this is completely practical: At that time purificators, the small cloths that are used to cleanse the cup, came into use, and white wine left fewer traces on them.

The bread and the wine must be in good condition. Care must be taken that "the wine does not turn to vinegar or the bread spoil or become too hard to be broken easily" (*GIRM* 285). The prayers of preparation close with a reference to their ultimate purpose: the bread and wine are to become the "bread of life" and "our spiritual drink."

Mixing Water with the Wine
Before the priest raises the chalice during the prayer of preparation, he pours a little water into the wine. This rite has its roots, first of all, in the custom of the classical world of not drinking wine that had not been mixed with water. Jesus quite probably followed this custom at the Last Supper. Beyond this, Christian tradition has seen various symbols in this action:

a) This is a reference to the blood and water that flowed from Christ's pierced side (John 19:34). This event was seen as symbolizing the birth of the Church and of the sacraments.

b) Wine and water became symbols of the divine and human natures in Christ. They were also seen as symbolizing our close relationship with Christ, which the New Testament describes as being members of the Body of Christ, even of participating in his divine nature (see 2 Pet 1:4). The prayer at the mixing of water and wine speaks of the wonderful exchange between Christ's divinity and our humanity: "By the mystery of this water and wine may we come to share in the divinity of Christ, who humbled himself to share in our humanity."

c) Another attractive symbol is found in the ancient Ethiopian liturgy, which contains the following statement in the "Anaphoras in Honor of Mary" from the eighth century: "As the water and wine in the chalice cannot be separated from each other, so never permit us to be separated from you and your Son, the Lamb of Salvation."

Additional Rites of Preparation

The offering of ourselves, which has already been discussed, finds its verbal expression in the following prayer for the acceptance of our offering of ourselves. Thereby we bind ourselves in solidarity with Christ's act of self-sacrifice. The priest prays it with bowed head not only for himself but also for all participants: "Lord God, we ask you to receive us and be pleased with the sacrifice we offer you with humble and contrite hearts." After this the gifts, the altar, the priest, and the people may be incensed. The prayers that formerly accompanied this action are no longer used.

In discussing the introductory rite, we described how incense is to be understood as a symbol of self-offering and prayer as well as of the Church's intercession and reverence (see above, p. 20). In our age widespread rationalism and dreary utilitarian thinking have made it difficult for many to accept such a rite. However, the fact remains that it can both assist and challenge us to comprehend the sacred event through meditation. At this time there are already many signs that the senses and emotions are once again demanding their proper place and that people are turning away from the coldness and dryness of worship that is too rationalized.

As a final rite in the preparation of the gifts, the priest washes his hands, an action that is also to be seen as part of the inner preparation of the faithful. Undoubtedly this was done for practical reasons in earlier times when the priest accepted gifts in their natural form. Today, however, it has an exclusively symbolic character. The accompanying prayer expresses this clearly: "Lord, wash away my iniquity; cleanse me from my sin."

Many religions have similar washings as external symbols of inner preparation for prayer and offering. In the celebration of the Mass, however, there is some reason to see this act as an unnecessary duplication of the penitential rite at the beginning of the liturgy and of the immediately preceding prayer of preparation asking for inner purity. Apparently, however, the group that had been assigned the reform of this part of the liturgy felt bound by tradition in enacting still one more purification rite before entering the holy of holies, as Psalm 24:3f. says:

"Who shall ascend the hill of the Lord?
And who shall stand in his holy place?
Those who have clean hands and pure hearts. . . ."

The Prayer over the Gifts

The preparation of the gifts concludes with the prayer over the gifts (*oratio super oblata*). Beginning in the eighth century in Gallic and French territories, this prayer was spoken softly and as a result became known as the "secret." The Latin *oratio secreta* means "a prayer spoken in a low voice." Some scholars, however, explain this name as being derived from the Latin *oratio super dona secreta*, meaning "a prayer over the gifts that have been set aside." It begins with the priest's invitation to prayer. The Roman Missal provides only the traditional prayer: *Orate, fratres . . .* ("Pray, brethren . . ."). Reference has already been made (above, pp. 52f.) to the fact that its two parts can easily lead to the misunderstanding that the sacrifice is already effected by the preparation of the gifts, whereas the prayer only asks for the acceptance of them.

The prayer over the gifts, which now follows, is, along with the opening prayer and the prayer after Communion, one of the presidential prayers. In contrast to earlier practice, the priest prays it aloud with outstretched arms. The constantly recurring motif is the petition that our gifts and prayers, and thus our self-offering, may be acceptable. On feast days frequent reference is made to the mystery being celebrated that day. Not infrequently the prayer refers to the central event that follows the prayer and prays that it will effect our salvation. Thus, for example, the prayer for the Twenty-sixth Sunday in Ordinary Time:

"God of mercy,
accept our offering
and make it a source of blessing for us."

Unfortunately many of the "texts of the prayer over the gifts that come from many different historical times . . . are far removed from being able to meet the standard (set by the General

Instruction—*GIRM* 53) of ending the preparation of the gifts and preparing for the Eucharistic Prayer."[21]

B. THE EUCHARISTIC PRAYER

In considering the Eucharistic Prayer, we enter into the innermost part of the celebration of the Eucharist. It begins with the dialogue before the preface and closes with the great doxology before the Our Father. Before we turn our attention to its texts and the corresponding rites, we must first deal with some basic questions.

The Meaning of the Eucharistic Prayer
The Eucharistic Prayer is a comprehensive prayer of thanks (Latin: *prex eucharistica*) for all God's saving acts, the greatest of which has become historical reality in the so-called paschal mystery. One of the texts of the New Testament describes this central saving act in precise terms and was used in the apostolic congregations as a hymn to Christ. It is in the Letter of Paul to the Philippians (2:6-11). The text reads as follows:

"Though he was in the form of God,
　[he] did not regard equality with God
　as something to be exploited,
but emptied himself, taking the form of a slave,
　being born in human likeness.
And being found in human form,
　he humbled himself
　and became obedient to the point of death—
　even death on a cross.
Therefore God also highly exalted him
　and gave him the name
　that is above every name,
so that at the name of Jesus
　every knee should bend,
　in heaven and on earth and under the earth,
and every tongue should confess
　that Jesus Christ is Lord,
　to the glory of God the Father."

[21] Hans B. Meyer, *Eucharistie: Geschichte, Theologie, Pastoral*, p. 344 (see note 1, chapter 1).

This hymn makes it clear that Jesus was not merely a teacher of wisdom and a courageous opponent of injustice and hypocrisy. He was also something other than what we in modern terms call a social revolutionary. Rather, he was the Son of God, of one being or substance with the Father, and the incarnation of God's love. In agreement with the saving will of his Father, he offered himself as the sacrificial lamb for the sins of the human race. His voluntary surrender to suffering and death on the cross became the redemptive sacrifice that established a new relationship between God and people. He is the unique sacrifice of the new covenant, which effects God's love through the Son in the Holy Spirit and abrogates all the religious sacrifices of the past.

Whoever participates in Jesus' loving surrender by voluntarily sharing his inner submission to the heavenly Father is admitted to fellowship with the triune God. For such a person, the curse of sin and the separation from God caused by sin have been overcome. We may, then, joyfully make the words of the hymn our own confession:

"Forsaken sinners we are no longer;
Redeemed Christians, rejoice;
Now we are God's children in Christ,
Participants in heavenly joy."[22]

At this point we must clearly reject the misunderstanding that Jesus' death on the cross was necessary in order to still the anger of a vengeful God. God is not a heartless tyrant who satisfies his need for vengeance with the blood of people. It is indeed true that God's holiness is diametrically opposed to sin; however, it is not God's nature to respond to sin with raging wrath but rather with constant love. This is what Jesus himself says: "For God so loved

[22] Wir sind nicht mehr verlassne Sünder;
erlöste Christen, freuet euch,
wir sind in Christus Gottes Kinder
und haben teil am Himmelreich.
—From the hymn "Mainz," written by Friedrich Spitta, 1899, on the basis of hymn by Johann Englisch, prior to 1530, in *Gotteslob* (edition for the diocese of Mainz), no. 916.

the world that he gave his only Son, so that everyone who believes in him may not perish but may have eternal life" (John 3:16). This is paralleled in the First Letter of John: "God's love was revealed among us in this way: God sent his only Son into the world so that we might live through him" (1 John 4:8). On the basis of these and similar statements in the Scriptures, we may rightly conclude:

"Therefore what takes place in the cross is the self-surrender of the Father through the Son and the self-surrender of the Son to the Father for the benefit of people. . . . The Son of the Father did not need to die in order to reconcile a distant God and to quench the heat of his wrath. Rather, this is all that is needed because it is only God who can reconcile people with God."[23]

However, God's Son, being one in love with the Father, has effected this reconciliation because he sacrificed his life not only for friends (see John 15:13) but also for the enemies of God. No clearer revelation of God's suprahuman love for people is possible.

The documents of Vatican II frequently refer to this central saving act as the "paschal mystery" (Latin: *mysterium paschale*) of Christ. The first document of the Council, the Constitution on the Sacred Liturgy, already used the Latin expression seven times.[24] The conciliar documents use the term "mystery" to mean something more than "secret." "Mystery" describes God's gracious activity in people which is beyond all human understanding. In this liturgical meaning, "mystery" is the unfathomable saving work of God.

The word "paschal" has its roots in the Hebrew word *pesach*, which literally means "passing over" and "passing through." As used here, it means Jesus's passing through his self-emptying, suffering, and death to resurrection. He has thereby made it possible for people to pass through darkness into light, through death into life, through the bondage of sin into the freedom of the children of God.

[23] Gerhard Ludwig Müller, *Lasst uns mit ihm gehen*, p. 159.
[24] See *SC* 5, 6 (twice), 104, 106, 107, 109.

The great Old Testament type of this paschal experience was the redemption of Israel from bondage in Egypt, the avenging angel's passing over the houses of the Israelites, their march through the Sea of Reeds, their experience of great need while wandering through the wilderness, and their entrance into the Promised Land.

The paschal mystery of Christ was a unique historical event. It is part of the past. While historical events sometimes have long-lasting effects, it is not possible to transplant them out of the past into the present. The situation is quite different with the paschal mystery of Christ. Beneath the veil of the sacramental signs, it becomes real presence. As often as the congregation follows the command Jesus gave at his Last Supper, "Do this in memory of me," the risen Christ becomes present, together with his self-giving love, his obedience to suffering, his will to save, and his intercession for all people. Hidden under the visible signs of bread and wine, he is present as the high priest of the new covenant with his body given for us, his blood shed for us.

Thus the Eucharistic Prayer is not merely a grateful act of remembrance, not even the remembrance of a past saving act, but rather a real encounter with the Christ who actively works our salvation. The Council of Trent followed the uninterrupted tradition of faith when it described this as a "re-presentation" of the one sacrifice of Christ that places it into the present as a contemporary reality. This is immediately combined with the "application," with the imparting of the fruit of salvation to all who permit themselves to be drawn into Christ's surrender.

Perhaps the two following comparisons will help us visualize this mystery of faith. Our sun constantly generates an abundance of light and warming energy, in all centuries, on all continents, on every city, and on every village. It has done so for millions of years without becoming noticeably weaker or losing its brightness. In a similar way, Christ, together with his paschal mystery, is a new kind of sun of salvation. This new sun shines wherever an assembly of believers is gathered together to remember his sacrifice and thereby opens itself in faith and love. This is an especially intense fulfillment of his promise: "Where two or three are gathered in my name, I am there among them" (Matt 18:20).

One of the wall paintings in the Roman catacombs depicts a man striking a wall of rock with his staff and a great spring of water coming out of the wall. This man first represents Moses, who worked this miracle by the power of God during Israel's wandering in the wilderness. For the faithful, however, Moses was only the example and pattern of Christ, the New Testament leader of God's people. On the rock of Golgotha he opened the spring from which redemption flows. He causes this spring to break through wherever his community gathers together to celebrate the Eucharist.

Only those who believe can grasp this sacramental re-presentation of Christ's sacrifice. It is a *mysterium fidei*, a "mystery of faith." Whoever views this saving event through the eyes of faith is not surprised that believers of past generations attempted to emphasize the value of this hidden and secret mystery with special symbols: the entrance procession with torches, incensation, the elevation of the host and the chalice after the institution narrative, polyphonic choral and instrumental music, kneeling in reverence, bowing deeply, making the sign of the cross, beating one's breast, sacred silence, and, in the Eastern Church, cautiously concealing the "terrifying mystery" behind the iconostasis (the screen decorated with icons separating the sanctuary from the rest of the church) and the "sacred gates."

All such forms of reverence express the piety of their time and are therefore open to change. They may not be understood as a law for all time to come, especially since they sometimes are based on an imperfect and wrongly emphasized understanding of the Eucharistic event. What is decisive for every age is the measure of faith and readiness to become part of Christ's loving surrender of himself to the Father.

The Eucharist as the Sacrifice of the Church
In God's new covenant with people, there is only one sacrifice that takes away the sins of the world once and for all—the sacri-

fice of Christ (see Rom 6:10; Heb 9:2ff.; 10:10; 1 Pet 3:18). The Old Testament regulations prescribing religious sacrifice have been abrogated. Now the question arises: How can the Eucharistic celebration still be called the sacrifice of the Church? This term appears not only in numerous liturgical texts but also in a dogmatic proclamation of the Council of Trent.[25]

The gifts of bread and wine cannot be this sacrifice, as we have already seen in the discussion of the preparation of the gifts (see above, pp. 52f.). As the psalm says, these are in the final analysis God's gifts that he provides to us people: "The earth is the Lord's and all that is in it" (Ps 24:1). An ecumenical council could never have intended to make a statement that would call into question the unique character of Christ's sacrifice.

For this reason the Eucharistic celebration can only be a sacrifice if it is in some way identical with Christ's once-for-all-time sacrifice that is sacramentally present under the form of the meal of bread and wine. The Church allows itself, through an act of inner surrender, to be taken into the Christ who sacrifices himself, and is thereby joined to this Christ in inner solidarity. This Church, which is now the Body of Christ, brings itself together with him as an offering to the Father. Christ is and remains the real priest who offers this sacrifice. Christ, however, acts in union with his Mystical Body, the Church. In the same way, Christ himself is the sacrificial offering, but also in union with his Mystical Body. To this extent, and only to this extent, may we say that the sacramentally re-presented sacrifice of Christ is also the sacrifice of the Church.

This understanding of the sacrifice in no way deviates from the teaching of the Church. This is demonstrated by the instruction of the Congregation on Rites published on May 25, 1967, entitled "Instruction on Eucharistic Worship" (*Eucharisticum Mysterium*). Its preface refers to various documents of Vatican II and then states:

"The celebration of the eucharist at Mass is the action not only of Christ but also of the Church. It is Christ's act because, perpetuat-

[25] Twenty-second session (September 17, 1562), canon 1.

ing in an unbloody way the sacrifice consummated on the cross, he offers himself to the Father for the salvation of the world through the ministry of priests. It is the Church's act because, as the Bride and minister of Christ exercising together with him the role of priest and victim, the Church offers him to the Father and at the same time completely offers itself together with him."[26]

The Church united with Christ is the people of God. All the baptized and confirmed belong to this body in the fullest way. Now it is the task of each individual Christian to join with this self-sacrifice of the Church through surrendering himself or herself in harmony with Christ's act of surrender. Thus the Mass not only becomes the sacrifice of the Church but also the sacrifice of each individual participant in the Eucharistic celebration.

"Offering the immaculate victim, not only through the hands of the priest but also with him, they should learn to offer themselves. Through Christ, the Mediator, they should be drawn day by day into ever more perfect unity with God and each other, so that finally God may be all in all" (SC 48).

The insistent urging of St. Paul is to be understood in this same sense: "I appeal to you therefore, brothers and sisters, by the mercies of God, to present your bodies as a living sacrifice, holy and acceptable to God, which is your spiritual worship" (Rom 12:1). The following verse interprets the meaning of this self-sacrifice: "Do not be conformed to this world, but be transformed by the renewing of your minds, so that you may discern what is the will of God—what is good and acceptable and perfect."

Such a view of the Eucharist is well suited to setting aside the misunderstandings of separated Christians and to leading to reconciliation. This has already become clear in numerous ecumenical conversations and documents.

The Different Forms of the Eucharistic Prayer
"Now the center and summit of the entire celebration begins: the eucharistic prayer, a prayer of thanksgiving and sanctification" (GIRM 54).

[26] DOL, p. 397.

From the beginning on, there was no single text of the Eucharistic Prayer; rather, a variety of forms developed. The oldest of the traditional Eucharistic Prayers used in the Church of Rome is recorded by the Roman priest Hippolytus and was written down about 215 (see above, pp. 7–8). Hippolytus, however, understood the text of his prayer as an outline. He explicitly recognized the right of every bishop to freely compose other texts, as long as these remained faithful to the traditions of the faith. Thus it is not surprising that his model experienced many changes and additions within the Roman Church itself. In fact, it is difficult to still recognize the original.

These changes occurred particularly during the transition from the use of Greek to the use of Latin as the language of the liturgy. This change took place during the second half of the fourth century. A definite form of the Eucharistic Prayer developed only gradually, reaching a kind of conclusion under Pope Gregory the Great (590–604). This was the "Roman Canon," which, with some changes, continued to be the standard until Vatican II. In any case, the history of the liturgy of the Mass clearly demonstrates that ecclesiastical authorities have changed both the form and the wording of this prayer without contradicting Christ's institution of the sacrament.

Since the eighth century the opinion has gradually developed that the Canon begins only after the *Sanctus*. This opinion was graphically demonstrated in Missals by drawing the first letters of the prayer after the *Sanctus (Te igitur)* as large capitals, and later by including a full-page illustration of the crucifixion at this point. In this way the preface and the *Sanctus* were separated out, and the praise and thanksgiving in the Eucharistic Prayer were thereby reduced to a minimum. This was certainly the greatest deficiency of the Roman Canon.

After Vatican II the attempt was made to reform this Roman Canon with its numerous intercessions and its weak elements of praise and thanks. It became clear that this attempt was simply impossible. Therefore Pope Paul VI in 1968 agreed to a proposal to provide three new Eucharistic Prayers as options alongside the text of an only slightly modified Roman Canon. As a result, the new Roman Missal of 1970 contains four Eucharistic Prayers.

Eucharistic Prayer I (Roman Canon). Apart from minor modifications (enclosing four conclusions for individual prayers in parentheses and shortening the list of saints), the form of the words of institution and the following acclamations, given in all four Eucharistic Prayers, are introduced. As far as changes in the ritual are concerned, the twenty-five signs of the cross used earlier are now reduced to one, and the two kisses of the altar are eliminated.

Eucharistic Prayer II. This is a reworking and revision of the Eucharistic Prayer of Hippolytus. The *Sanctus*, missing in Hippolytus' text, and an epiclesis of the Holy Spirit are added. The order of some sections has also been changed. With reference to its source, it has been called the "Eucharistic Prayer from the time of the martyrs."[27]

Eucharistic Prayer III. This is a new creation based on a proposal of the Italian liturgical scholar Cipriano Vagaggini. It is distinguished primarily by the way in which it arranges the individual structural elements in an organic and clear manner. In so doing, it does not merely rely on the Roman Canon but also incorporates ideas and texts from the liturgy and theological tradition. It has no preface of its own.

Eucharistic Prayer IV. This Eucharistic Prayer draws heavily on the traditions of the Eastern Church (the *Apostolic Constitutions* of Antioch and the Byzantine Liturgy of St. Basil). It contains a preface that is never changed and, beginning at this point, extends the thanksgiving in praise of God's acts of salvation through the *Sanctus* to the paschal mystery of Christ and the sending of the Holy Spirit. It then moves on through the epiclesis of the Holy Spirit to the account of the institution of this sacrament. This comprehensive praise of the history of salvation is like a confession that praises the whole Christian faith. The use of this Eucharistic

[27] Theodor Schnitzler, *Die drei neuen eucharistischen Hochgebete und die neue Präfationen. In Verkündigung und Betrachtung* (Freiburg: Herder, 1968), p. 25.

Prayer in a Mass in which the Creed is also used would result in undesirable duplication.

In addition to these three new Eucharistic Prayers, three Eucharistic Prayers for Masses with Children and two Eucharistic Prayers for Masses of Reconciliation are now available. Switzerland and Austria have additional Eucharistic Prayers on this theme. Switzerland also has another Eucharistic Prayer composed on the occasion of its Synod of Bishops in 1974. This contains four variations and has also been adopted in some other countries. As early as 1970, a Eucharistic Prayer for Masses with the Deaf of German-speaking regions was published. This contains simplified language and is also suitable for use with the developmentally disabled.

Since 1967 numerous private versions of the Eucharistic Prayer have also been published alongside the official Eucharistic Prayers. These have come primarily from the Netherlands and have been widely disseminated. The bishops have on several occasions forbidden their use. At the same time the bishops have asked the officials in Rome to permit new Eucharistic Prayers. However, a circular letter of the Sacred Congregation for Divine Worship issued on April 27, 1973, gave the bishops only the possibility of approving and permitting new prefaces and insertions.[28]

Undoubtedly every age has the right to praise God out of its awareness of its own living faith and in its own language. On the other hand, the approval of liturgical texts by the leaders of the Church is necessary. The need for obtaining such approval will help to ensure that the "source and summit" of Christian worship will not be falsified by the subjective one-sidedness of a given period of history.

The Important Elements of the Eucharistic Prayer
The nature of the Eucharistic Prayer and its focus on real historical events can be recognized on the basis of its most important elements. The General Instruction of the Roman Missal names the following: thanksgiving, as especially expressed in the preface; the

[28] Circular letter *Eucharistiae Participationem,* on the Eucharistic Prayers (*DOL,* pp. 623ff.).

acclamation of the *Sanctus;* the epiclesis, or invocation of the Holy
Spirit; the institution narrative and consecration; anamnesis
(remembering); offering; intercessions; and concluding doxology
(*GIRM* 55). In the following pages we will discuss each of these
in detail, with special reference to whether and in what form they
appear in each of the four Eucharistic Prayers of the Missal.

The Preface

All the Eucharistic Prayers begin with a prayer in the form of a
three-part dialogue between the priest and the congregation. This
dialogue refers not only to the following preface but also to the
entire Eucharistic Prayer. In its texts we encounter material from
ancient Jewish and Christian prayers. It both invokes and expresses deep gratitude and remembrance. To do that, we need
God's help. For without God we are not able to do anything (see
John 15:5). That is why the priest greets the congregation with the
wish "The Lord be with you." The congregation prays the same
for the priest when it answers. In the Orthodox liturgy the priest
prays a slightly changed version of Paul's final prayer in the Second Letter to the Corinthians (13:13): "The grace of the Lord Jesus
Christ, the love of God, and the communion of the Holy Spirit be
with all of you."

Our entry into the most holy place of the celebration of the Eucharist requires us to be open and prepared to receive the divine
mystery. Experience teaches us that we humans still are glued to
the floor even in the most sacred moments of life, that is, we remain trapped in our daily thoughts and cares. Now, however, we
need to free ourselves from all the chains that bind us. Therefore
we are told: "Lift up your hearts" (*Sursum corda*). Even in the
earliest life of the Church, theologians ascribed great meaning to
this summons. It is that attitude which the apostolic letters repeatedly require (see Col 3:1f. and Phil 3:20). The response of the congregation, "We lift them to the Lord," builds the transition to the
last prayer prayed alternately:

"Let us give thanks to the Lord our God.
It is right to give him thanks and praise."

The remembering of God's great acts in creation and redemption leads us to give thanks. Anyone who thinks also thanks. When the Mass is celebrated with small groups and with children, the participants themselves may express their reasons for praise and thanks at this point. This provides the possibility of a very personal witness to our faith. The congregation responds affirmatively to the summons to give thanks with an acclamation that was frequently used in earlier times: "It is right to give him thanks and praise."

The preface follows this three-part dialogical prayer. It is the first prayer of thanks and praise. When the word "preface" is used in the liturgy, it does not mean something that is spoken before something else; rather, the first syllable, "pre," is to be understood in a spatial sense: The priest, *before* God and the congregation, "praises the Father and gives thanks to him for the whole work of salvation or for some special aspect of it that corresponds to the day, feast, or season" (*GIRM* 55a). The preface thus expresses the main theme of the Eucharistic Prayer, that is, the giving of thanks. In so doing it picks up on the last words of the preceding dialogue: "We do well always and everywhere to give you thanks."

In the Leonine Sacramentary, the oldest sacramentary of the Western Church (about 550), each celebration of the Mass had its own preface. There were 267 different prefaces. Since there was much chaff among them, Gregory the Great (590–604) decided to radically shorten this list, leaving only fourteen. Under Charlemagne and his successors, the number was reduced to seven. Before the year 1000 the prefaces on the themes of the cross, the Trinity, and preparation for fasting were added. At the end of the eleventh century, a preface focusing on Mary was added. There were now eleven prefaces, and there was no further expansion until the twentieth century, when five more were added: the preface in memory of the dead (1919); for St. Joseph (1919); for Christ the King (1925); for the Sacred Heart (1928); and finally the preface for the Chrism Mass on Holy Thursday. In 1968 the Sacred Congregation of Rites published eight new prefaces at the same time that it published the three new Eucharistic Prayers. The Roman Missal of 1970 finally increased this number to over eighty.

Every preface consists of three parts: the introduction, the glorification of the particular work of salvation that is specially remembered in the Mass being celebrated, and the transition to the congregational song, the *Sanctus*. If one were to gather together the middle sections of all the prefaces and arrange them in order, one would have a complete, although brief, overview of God's saving work. One would also have a summary of all that we believe, together with its radiations into the Christian life. Because this deals with real proclamation, we can understand how much was lost pastorally when this material was covered with two veils: first by the Latin, which most people did not understand, and then by the priest's speaking this prayer inaudibly (in the so-called silent Masses). Since 1965 the Eucharistic Prayer may be spoken aloud, and since 1967, in the language of the people.

As far as the choice of prefaces in the individual celebrations of the Mass is concerned, Eucharistic Prayer IV has an unchangeable preface. Eucharistic Prayers I and III have no preface of their own. We are, therefore, free to choose a given preface, as long as this choice is not limited by the special character of the Mass (feasts, defined seasons, saints' days). This is also true of Eucharistic Prayer II, of which the General Instruction says: "Although it has its own preface, it may also be used with other prefaces, especially those that summarize the mystery of salvation . . ." (*GIRM* 322b). A later instruction also is worth mentioning: "A eucharistic prayer that has its own preface may be used with that preface, when the Mass calls for the preface of the season" (*GIRM* 322e).

The Acclamation of the Sanctus
While the middle section of the prefaces describes God's saving acts, the last sentence is a transition to the acclamation of the *Sanctus*, the great song of God's glory, which the Eucharistic assembly sings in fellowship with the choirs of angels. It consists of two sections of text, each of which is closely related to a passage of the Bible.

The first part is related to the calling of the prophet Isaiah. In a vision he sees the Lord on his throne, surrounded by seraphim with six wings, who call to one another: "Holy, holy, holy is the Lord of hosts; the whole earth is full of his glory" (Isa 6:3).

The second part adopts the shouts of praise spoken by the crowds of people when Jesus entered Jerusalem on Palm Sunday. Matthew reports the greeting of the crowd as: "Hosanna to the Son of David! Blessed is the one who comes in the name of the Lord! Hosanna in the highest heaven!" (Matt 21:9).

The acclamation of the *Sanctus* is thus based on Scripture. Its first part glorifies the all-holy God, whose glory fills heaven and earth. The Hebrew word *Hosanna* in the second section is not translated in the Gospels. It originally meant "Pray, save (us)." However, it very soon became an acclamation glorifying and praising God. That is how it is used in our text. Combined with the "in the highest (*in excelsis*)," it is a clear reminder of the angels' song *Gloria in excelsis Deo*.

This acclamation of praise also applies to the Son of God "who comes in the name of the Lord." His coming becomes a saving presence in the celebration of the Eucharist. It is not merely that he came and will come again, but his "advent" occurs in this very hour.

Unfortunately many congregations neither speak nor sing this venerable text any longer but rather replace it with a more or less successful "*Sanctus* song." This is done even though it is not permitted to choose any popular song of praise as a replacement.[29] It would certainly be a significant loss, both pastorally and liturgically, if the textual form of this great biblical song were to disappear from the awareness of the faithful because some other song had been regularly substituted for it.

Richer melodies were developed at the end of the Middle Ages, and finally polyphonic compositions of significant length were created. Along with these developments came the abuse by which

[29] See *DOL*, p. 483, R15; *Music in Catholic Worship*, p. 23.

the priest proceeded with the quiet praying of the Canon during the presentation of the *Sanctus.* The institution narrative as well as the elevations and the following sections of the liturgy even took place while the *Sanctus* was being sung. As a result the Ceremonial for Bishops of 1600 prescribed that the elevation could take place only after the first *Hosanna,* and the section of the *Hosanna* beginning "Blessed" (*Benedictus*) was to be sung after the elevations. Such a harmful division of the acclamation of the *Sanctus* is no longer permitted, since the reform of the liturgy has specified that the Eucharistic Prayer is to be spoken out loud.

The new Eucharistic Prayers, in contrast to Eucharistic Prayer I, contain an organic transition from the *Sanctus* to the following prayers. One may even speak of the section following the *Sanctus* as the "post-*Sanctus*." In Eucharistic Prayer II this consists of the single sentence: "Lord, you are holy indeed, the fountain of all holiness." Eucharistic Prayer III does this more extensively by referring to the creation filled with life and grace:

". . . all creation rightly gives you praise.
All life, all holiness comes from you . . ."

and to the assembly of the new people of God:

"From age to age you gather a people to yourself,
so that from east to west
a perfect offering may be made
to the glory of your name" [see Mal 1:11].

In Eucharistic Prayer IV the praise of God extends in great detail even after the *Sanctus.*

The Missal provides several texts that can be inserted after the post-*Sanctus.* In Eucharistic Prayer I these texts commemorating the saints (which start in Latin with the word *Communicantes* and are often referred to by this title) can be inserted only in connection with the commemoration of the saints. These texts are related to the particular mystery being celebrated on this feast. They praise God for specific saving acts and thereby form an organic extension of the praise in the preface and the *Sanctus.* The old

Roman Canon in the earlier Roman Missal and in the present text of Eucharistic Prayer I offers six special forms of the *Communicantes* and does so in connection with the commemorating of the saints (*Communicantes propria*).

The Epiclesis Asking for the Change of the Elements

"Epiclesis" is a Greek word that has been taken over into English and means an invocation of God, especially of the Holy Spirit, concerning a person or a thing that is thereby consecrated. In the context of the Eucharistic Prayer it is a prayer for the change of bread and wine. In Eucharistic Prayers II and III it follows immediately after the post-*Sanctus*. It is also possible to recognize an epiclesis in Eucharistic Prayer I; it is found in the prayer immediately before the institution narrative, even though the Holy Spirit is not explicitly named.

In Eucharistic Prayer IV the epiclesis comes only after a long praise of the events of salvation history and the mention of the sending of the Holy Spirit on Pentecost: "to complete his work on earth and bring us the fullness of grace." Thus it is God who, through the Holy Spirit, works the miracle of the change. Understood in this way, the epiclesis "removes every suspicion of magic from the Eucharist, as though human effort or power were able to prepare the Eucharistic gifts."[30] We may therefore speak of the priest's power to bring about a change of the elements only with great caution. What the priest accomplishes as an agent of the Church through the Eucharistic Prayer is only the presupposition for the work of divine omnipotence.

In most of the Eastern liturgies, this epiclesis asking for the change of the gifts comes after the words of institution and the anamnesis. This difference ignited a serious controversy in the early Middle Ages. Western theologians thought of the change of the gifts as resulting from the institution narrative, whereas Eastern theologians ascribed this to the epiclesis. The last words of the epiclesis are: "and change them through your Holy Spirit."

[30] Manfred Probst, "*Das neue Hochgebet und die verschiedenen Texte*, in *Gemeinde im Herrenmahl. Zur Praxis der Messfeier*, 2nd ed., ed. Theodor Mass-Ewerd and Klemens Richter, (Freiburg: Herder, 1976), p. 292.

Today, however, as in the first four centuries, theologians again emphasize the unity of the Eucharistic Prayer. As a result this controversy has begun to subside, at least in the West.

The last words of the Western epiclesis asking for the change of the elements are accompanied by two gestures of blessing: the priest joins his hands and extends them over the gifts and blesses them by making the sign of the cross.

The Institution Narrative
This is the essential part of the Eucharistic Prayer, most closely relating it to the source of the Eucharistic sacrament in the Last Supper of Jesus. As we stated above (pp. 2–3), the New Testament contains four versions of this event. Many readers may be surprised to learn that the text used in the Roman liturgy does not literally correspond to the biblical accounts. Renowned scholars such as Josef Jungmann have reached the conclusion that the liturgical version of the institution narrative is even older than the New Testament texts. They assert that it is based on a tradition that is very close to the original:

"Here we face an outgrowth of the fact that the Eucharist was celebrated long before the evangelists and St. Paul set out to record the Gospel story. Even the glaring discrepancies in the biblical texts themselves regarding this very point are explained by this fact. For in them we evidently find segments from the liturgical life of the first generation of Christians."[31]

However, since the liturgical texts were still very much in flux, this original institution narrative was partially changed to conform to the various biblical institution narratives. This is also the case in the Eastern liturgies. All this makes it clear that the Christians of the first centuries were not so much concerned with an unchangeable sentence structure and vocabulary as with agreement on the content. For this reason people in the East were never concerned about the differing formulations used in individual liturgies and never doubted that such variations were permissible and varying liturgies were valid.

[31] Josef A. Jungmann, *The Mass of the Roman Rite*, p. 418.

The framework of the text of the liturgical institution narrative also varies in the four Eucharistic Prayers of the new Roman Missal. However, it was the special concern of Pope Paul VI that the words of institution should be the same in all Eucharistic Prayers:

"Take this, all of you, and eat it:
this is my body which will be given up for you."

"Take this, all of you, and drink from it:
this is the cup of my blood,
the blood of the new and everlasting covenant.
It will be shed for you and for all
so that sins may be forgiven.
Do this in memory of me."

In this process the expression "the mystery of faith" was also separated from the old Roman Canon. Now the priest speaks it after the elevation of the chalice. It serves as the introduction to the following acclamation spoken by the congregation.

Corresponding to the Western tradition, the General Instruction continues to maintain that the words of institution are to be considered the real consecrating element: "In the words and actions of Christ, that sacrifice is celebrated which he himself instituted at the Last Supper . . ." (GIRM 55d). This is stated even more clearly in article 3 of the foreword, which was written later: "The celebration of Mass also proclaims the sublime mystery of the Lord's real presence under the eucharistic elements. . . . The Mass does this not only by means of the very words of consecration, by which Christ becomes present through transubstantiation . . ." (GIRM, Introduction, 3).

This identification of the change as taking place at the moment of consecration was not approved by all the fathers of the Council. Those fathers who belong to the Eastern Uniate Rites represented their traditional conviction that the change of the gifts takes place through the epiclesis (after the institution narrative and anamnesis). As earlier suggested (see above, pp. 77f.), this controversial problem can be solved only by referring to the character of the Eucharistic Prayer as a single totality.

The earliest elevation of the consecrated gifts occurred in the Roman Rite in connection with the final doxology of the Eucharistic Prayer. This custom is still followed today. The separate elevation of the host that is customary today immediately after the words of institution is first noted about the year 1200. The cause of this ritual was the great desire of the medieval faithful to see something happen. They expected to receive a special blessing because they had seen the elevated host. The elevation of the chalice developed somewhat later, and the Missal of Pius V (1570) made it a general requirement.

There is no binding rule that the bell be rung before the institution narrative and during both of the elevations; however, the General Instruction explicitly permits it (*GIRM* 109). The priest's reverential genuflection before and after the elevation became the usual custom only around 1500. The new Order of the Mass recognizes such a genuflection only after each elevation.

A very serious controversy arose concerning the translation of the words of institution into the language of the people (for example, German, English, Italian) in several of the Missals. In the Latin Missal it is stated that the blood of Christ is shed "for you and for many (*pro multis*)"; the vernacular missals stated this as "for you and for all." Some saw this as such a very serious corruption of the Latin text that it called the validity of such a celebration of the Mass into question.

In response, it must be said that Sacred Scripture and the teaching of the Church clearly state that God's will to save in and through Christ is universal, that is, it was Christ's intention to shed his blood for all. This is clearly demonstrated by passages such as Romans 8:31; 2 Corinthians 5:14f.; 1 Timothy 2:6; 1 John 2:2. John 6:51 contains a similar reference within the context of the Eucharistic address. Consequently, the translation "for all" is absolutely orthodox.

The fact that Mark and Matthew (who follows Mark in this regard) use the phrase "for many" in speaking of the cup is related to the nature of the Hebrew and Aramaic languages. These languages have no words for "all," and so they use the word "many" to describe "the great multitude," "the whole," that is, in the sense of "all." Although the Greek language does have a word for "all" and although Mark and Matthew were written in Greek, they still cling to this Hebrew way of speaking. However, they had no intention of denying that God wills to save all of humanity through Christ's sacrifice on the cross. Paul also uses the Greek word for "many" (*polloi*) in the sense of "all." Romans 5:12-18 and 1 Corinthians 15:22 clearly demonstrate this usage.

The Roman Missal preserves "for many" out of reverence for the Greek text of Matthew and Mark. For this reason this usage can be understood in an orthodox way as describing the actual effect of Christ's sacrifice rather than focusing on his universal saving intention. For the Catholic faith teaches that some people can actually lose salvation through their own fault.

In any case, it is absurd to view the vernacular translation "for all" as a corruption that calls into question the validity of the words of consecration and therewith the whole Mass.

These explanations of the words of institution would be incomplete if they did not propose some ideas about the way in which Christ is present under the signs of bread and wine. However, because we do not intend to offer here a dogmatic treatise, the reader is asked to understand that these problems and their attempted solutions can be discussed only briefly.

Jesus at the Last Supper says: "This is my body, which is given for you" (Luke 22:19). Hebrew-Aramaic usage indicates that he means in effect: "This is I, who sacrifice myself for you." The word spoken over the chalice has the same meaning: "This is I, who shed my blood as a sacrifice for you." Both statements of the institution narrative thus mean the same: Jesus is present together with his love and surrender in the gifts of this meal, in the bread and wine. As such he wishes to draw his disciples into his love and surrender, and will himself be received by them: "Take this, all of you, and eat (drink from) it." In this sacramental meal he wills to become one with them and with us.

81

The question, however, is: How can we describe the manner of his presence in bread and wine? Even at the time of the address promising the Eucharist that Jesus gave in Capernaum (John 6:32ff.), it was clear that many hearers grossly misunderstood what he said. "How can this man give us his flesh to eat?" (John 6:52). Apparently they imagined that they would have to eat a piece of his body and drink a swallow of the blood that was pulsing in his body. Like many of the disciples (John 6:60f.), some Christians in later centuries also were caught up in such ideas and involved in great difficulties with their faith. Such erroneous ideas about the sensual consumption of the body and blood of Christ have also been called "sensism" [*Sensualismus*].[32]

The Middle Ages attempted to achieve clarity by using the concept of "transubstantiation." The outward appearance of bread and wine with all their properties (accidents) are preserved. What is transformed is the invisible "substance," the substance or essence of bread and wine. As a result, people spoke of "transubstantiation." However, is the invisible essence of a material thing its "substance"? Today people who have been trained in modern physics understand the substance of a material thing to be its chemical-physical structure, the combination of certain molecules, all of which can be divided, studied, and changed. This chemical-physical structure is precisely what the Church's teaching asserts is not changed. Thus the concept of transubstantiation is of no use in proclaiming this faith today. It would simply evoke misunderstandings and contradictions.

For this reason more recent theology has attempted to clarify the Eucharistic mystery by using the new terms "transignification" (change of meaning) and "transfinalization" (change of purpose).

---

[32] The *New Catholic Encyclopedia*, vol. 13, p. 94a, defines "sensism": "A theory of knowledge holding that whatever is intelligible is also sensible. Sensists make sense perception the primary function of the cognitive process, and regard memory, imagination, and reasoning as activities of the same faculty that receives external sense perceptions. They tend to regard man as differing from other sentient beings only in degree." Some examples cited are Democritus, Lucretius, Hobbes, Locke, Hume, Comte, Mill, Reid, Spencer, G. B. Moore, B. Russell, and Freud.— *Trans.*

The natural meaning of bread and wine is that they are means of nourishment for people; their goal is to preserve and strengthen life. In the change that takes place in the Eucharist, bread or wine is removed from the context of its previous frame of reference and now serves as a means of unification with Christ. Thereby these natural foodstuffs receive a new meaning and new purpose.

"The term 'transignification' intends to say: The signs of bread and wine are given another function as signs through Jesus working in the power of his Holy Spirit. He changes their sign, and it is thus that we recognize and receive them through faith. His relationship to these gifts has been totally changed. Because of the change of the sign-character of bread and wine, this food is no longer merely physical nourishment, no longer only an expression of human fellowship, but rather the presence of his body. If we take the philosophical basis of these considerations seriously, transignification is not an addition to the concept of transubstantiation but rather a different way of describing the same event. . . . Transignification means not only that the reality of the food changes but rather the whole symbolic and faithful action of the Eucharistic congregation. This meal is now no longer a mere meal that satisfies hunger; it is also not only an expression of human fellowship among brothers and sisters. This meal itself is so transignified that it is now a sign, a sign that effectively brings about Christ's loving community with us on the basis of his offering of himself for us."[33]

Obviously this attempt at resolving the issues does not provide a satisfactory answer to every question. The sacrament of the Eucharist remains a "mystery of faith," whose depths even the sharpest human analysis will never be able to plumb. However, very many theologians have carefully evaluated the proposed interpretation and consider it the best available in our time. They cannot find any contradiction between it and the intention of the documents of the Council of Trent and of other teaching documents of the Church.

[33] Theodor Schneider, *Zeichen der Nähe Gottes. Grundriss der Sakramententheologie,* 6th ed. (Mainz-Weisenau: Matthias-Grünewald, 1992), pp. 164f.

The Acclamation
Whereas the Roman Canon until recently reserved to the priest
all the texts of the liturgy after the *Sanctus* through the Our
Father, the new Order of the Mass provides for an acclamation
spoken by the congregation after the words of institution. The
priest introduces it with "Let us proclaim the mystery of faith"
(which has been detached from its former place in the old Roman
Canon), and the congregation responds:

"Christ has died,
Christ is risen,
Christ will come again."

This text is based on 1 Corinthians 11:26. In it the congregation
confesses its thanks and praise for Christ's great work of salvation, the paschal mystery. This change makes it clear that the
whole congregation is involved in the celebration of the mystery
of Christ. This also has the desirable effect of loosening the mono-
logue prayer of the priest and thus makes it very clear that the
whole congregation is also involved in the celebration of Christ's
saving work. The Roman Missal contains three additional texts
that can be freely used as the text of the acclamation.

"Dying you destroyed our death,
rising you restored our life.
Lord Jesus, come in glory."

"When we eat this bread and drink this cup,
we proclaim your death, Lord Jesus,
until you come in glory."

"Lord, by your cross and resurrection
you have set us free.
You are the Savior of the world."

The Anamnesis (Memorial or Remembering)
The institution narratives of Luke (22:19) and Paul (1 Cor 11:24f.)
report the Lord's instructions that this meal of his body and blood
is to be held in the future. The words of institution, which are the

same in all the Eucharistic Prayers, repeat this command: "Do this in memory of me."

The congregation's acclamations have already remembered with praise and thanks the paschal mystery and Christ's coming again. This happens once again in the following prayer, the name of which is the Greek term *anamnesis*. The Eucharistic Prayers name specific phases of Christ's saving work: Eucharistic Prayer I refers to suffering, resurrection, and ascension; Eucharistic Prayer II refers to death and resurrection; Eucharistic Prayer III names suffering, resurrection, ascension, and coming again; Eucharistic Prayer IV adds the descent to the fathers ("his descent among the dead"). By faithfully participating in this conceptually detailed remembering (memorial), we encounter over and over the presence of the saving love of the triune God. The experience of this love gives new strength to our thankfulness and hope.

The Offertory Prayer
Following the anamnesis and closely related to it, the offertory prayer in the Eucharistic Prayers also includes the petition that the offering may be acceptable. This happens most extensively in Eucharistic Prayer I, the old Roman Canon:

"We offer to you, God of glory and majesty,
this holy and perfect sacrifice:
the bread of life
and the cup of eternal salvation."

This is followed by the petition for the acceptance of the offering, in which God is reminded of the well-pleasing offerings of Abel, Abraham, and Melchizedek. This petition uses the daring imagery of the holy angels in expressing the hope that they will bring these gifts of the offering to the heavenly altar:

"Almighty God,
we pray that your angel may take this sacrifice
to your altar in heaven."

The offering prayer is considerably shorter in Eucharistic Prayer II. There it is combined with the anamnesis into a single sentence:

"We offer you, Father, this life-giving bread,
this saving cup."

Eucharistic Prayer III clearly defines what the "holy and living
sacrifice" of the Eucharist is:

"Look with favor on your Church's offering,
and see the Victim whose death has reconciled us to yourself."

The self-surrender of each individual Christian must be combined
with this sacrifice of Christ:

"May he make us an everlasting gift to you
and enable us to share in the inheritance of your saints."

Finally, Eucharistic Prayer IV, in conjunction with the offertory
prayer and the prayer for acceptance, speaks of each participant
becoming "a living sacrifice of praise."

Earlier (see above, p. 68) we explained that the Church as the
Body of Christ and every Christian as a member of this Body must
be closely joined with this sacrifice of Christ, not with words but
rather in surrender to the will of the heavenly Father, in harmony
with Christ's surrender. This "self-offering" of the Church and of
each individual Christian takes place particularly in the offertory
prayer.

Indeed, Paul had already demanded such a self-offering in the
Letter to the Romans (12:1), describing it as "holy and acceptable
to God . . . your spiritual worship." Of course, Paul was describing a basic way of thinking about the entire lifestyle of Christians
as a living sacrifice. However, we should not therefore conclude
that he was not also thinking specifically of the Eucharistic
celebration. Indeed, it is more than likely that Paul's language
specifically refers to the basic components of participating in the
Eucharistic celebration.

Actually, the Letter to the Romans was written only a few months
after the First Letter to the Corinthians, a letter in which Paul
speaks about the Eucharist in response to a specific situation. Because it is a participation in the body and blood of Christ and a

deepening of membership in the Mystical Body (see 1 Cor 10:16f.), he severely condemns the egoistic behavior of many members of the congregation who do not hesitate to humiliate the poor at the Eucharistic gatherings and let them go hungry while they themselves feast and get drunk (1 Cor 11:20-22). All who celebrate the Eucharist must free themselves from all egoism and present themselves to God as "a living and holy sacrifice" (Rom 12:1).

Offering ourselves to God specifically means submitting to God's will without reservation; growing in love of God and of neighbor; walking the way of the cross in our own lives and offering up this life under the cross not only for the salvation of our own souls but also for the temporal and eternal welfare of all. All this is part of being conformed to Christ's redeeming offering of himself. It must determine the nature of our life even after the celebration of the Eucharist, as Ephesians 4:22-24 says: "You were taught to put away your former way of life, your old self, corrupt and deluded by its lusts, and to be renewed in the spirit of your minds, and to clothe yourselves with the new self, created according to the likeness of God in true righteousness and holiness."

This inner reshaping of our lives in the context of the Eucharistic celebration has been properly described as the inner change of the participants that must follow the change of the bread and wine. What is at stake here is becoming more completely like Christ in the power of the Holy Spirit and becoming more deeply incorporated into the Mystical Body of Christ. After all, as people who have been called by God, we are "predestined to be conformed to the image of his Son, in order that he might be the firstborn within a large family" (Rom 8:29).

The Epiclesis Asking for the Fruits of Communion
In all four Eucharistic Prayers there is a petition closely related to the offertory prayer that has been called the epiclesis of Communion. The epiclesis before the institution narrative asks for the change of the elements; this petition asks that the receiving of the changed gifts may so change the participants that they become more closely joined to Christ and therefore to salvation. This is how Eucharistic Prayer I puts it:

"Then, as we receive from this altar
the sacred body and blood of your Son,
let us be filled with every grace and blessing."

The epiclesis asking for the fruits of Communion in Eucharistic Prayer II reads:

"May all of us who share in the body and blood of Christ
be brought together in unity by the Holy Spirit."

Eucharistic Prayer III leads us to pray:

"Grant that we, who are nourished by his body and blood,
may be filled with his Holy Spirit,
and become one body, one spirit in Christ."

In Eucharistic Prayer IV we pray:

". . . by your Holy Spirit, gather all who share
this one bread and one cup
into the one body of Christ . . . ."

Thus, already in the Eucharistic Prayer our attention is focused on the real high point of the Eucharistic celebration—on the command to "eat" and to "drink."

The Intercessions
In accordance with the thinking of the early Christians, the Eucharistic Prayer is primarily thanksgiving and praise for God's saving works. Thus it is understandable that at the time of the reform of the Mass, many expressed the wish that the intercessions would be completely omitted from the Eucharistic Prayer. This seemed all the more appropriate because the restoration of the "prayer of the faithful" provided broad opportunity for such intercessions. These people were also not very happy with the way intercessions are interspersed so frequently throughout the traditional Roman Canon that the praise and thanksgiving are reduced to a minimum. All this made it understandable that there was a certain reservation regarding the intercessory remembrances in the new Eucharistic Prayers.

On the other hand, such wishes to dispense with intercessions in the Eucharistic Prayer

"are contrary to very early liturgical tradition (even though not as early as Hippolytus of Rome). The model underlying the Eucharistic Prayers is that of the Jewish Berakah and the mature forms of that prayer make the transition from praise to intercession. Similarly the new versions of the Eucharistic Prayer produced by Anglicans, Lutherans, Reformed, and other Christians do not eliminate this element. Because of their meaning in the context of the Eucharistic Prayers, these intercessions are not, strictly speaking, duplicates of the intentions of the prayer of the faithful but rather an expression of communion."[34]

These intercessions are different from those of the prayer of the faithful. They are not spoken "for public authorities and the salvation of the world" or "for those oppressed by any need" (GIRM 46) but rather are primarily concerned with the Church as a whole and the Eucharistic community in particular.

The inner basis for the inclusion of these intercessions lies, however, in a basic law of Christian prayer:

"A Christian can never offer a longer prayer of thanksgiving to God without almost automatically also trusting in being able to depend on God's help in the future. A prayer of thanksgiving that omits such petitions could give the impression of merely fulfilling a duty. The omission of the petitions would seem to be an expression of pride. The salvation that God brings is, as long as people on earth have reason to give thanks, never complete."[35]

Finally, we may not overlook the fact that Christ is present with the Father as our mediator. The priest who celebrates the Eucharist "in the person [persona]" of Christ now takes his place at

[34] Emil J. Lengeling, Die neue Ordnung der Eucharistiefeier (Münster: Regensberg, 1970), p. 23.
[35] Rainer Kaczynski, "Die Interzessionen im Hochgebet," in Gemeinde im Herrenmahl. Zur Praxis der Messfeier, 2nd ed., ed. Theodor Mass-Ewerd and Klemens Richter, Freiburg: Herder, 1976), p. 308.

the side of him who continually intercedes for us with the Father (see Heb 7:25; 9:24).

"The intercessions of the Eucharistic Prayer are the Church's way of participating in the continuous intercession that Christ offers because of his sacrifice. Just as the sacrifice that the Church celebrates is Christ's sacrifice, so the Church's intercessions are the intercessions of Christ."[36]

The intercessions of Eucharistic Prayer II are given as an example of the memorial petitions. Our consideration of their form in the other Eucharistic Prayers will be based on these:

"Lord, remember your Church throughout the world;
make us grow in love,
together with N. our Pope,
N. our bishop, and all the clergy.

They are thus a prayer for the whole people of God, especially for its officials and all who minister in the service of the Church. On certain days and for certain occasions, the circle of those who are named in particular can be expanded. This can be done from Easter Eve to Whitsunday,[37] for the newly baptized at a Mass combined with baptism, as well as for the newly confirmed at the Mass at which confirmation is administered, and for the newly married couple at a nuptial Mass. Rome authorized the regional conferences of bishops to add other occasions to this list.

Eucharistic Prayer I provides such a memorial petition for the whole Church and its ministers already in the first prayer after the *Sanctus (Te igitur)*. Eucharistic Prayer III expands this petition to include "the entire people your Son has gained for you," including all of those who are part of the Church. Eucharistic Prayer IV

---

[36] Ibid., 309.

[37] The author uses the German term that is literally translated as "White Sunday," corresponding to the English contraction "Whitsunday." This Sunday is more commonly referred to as "Pentecost." Adam's usage of Whitsunday here is deliberate and refers to the custom of the early Church that the newly baptized received white robes at Easter when they were baptized and wore them until "White Sunday."—*Trans.*

explicitly includes "all who seek you with a sincere heart." At this point we see something of the catholicity expressed by Christ in the command sending his disciples to carry out his mission (Matt 28:19f.).

The second intercession in Eucharistic Prayer II is made on behalf of "our brothers and sisters who have gone to their rest in the hope of rising again." Before this petition the names of the particular deceased for whom this Mass is being celebrated may be inserted.

When the dead are remembered in Eucharistic Prayer I, the German Missal explicitly provides that the priest and the congregation may spend "a brief period of silent prayer for the departed who are commemorated."[38] This silent remembering can and should also take place in the other Eucharistic Prayers. Experience shows that the congregations are thankful for this opportunity. Eucharistic Prayer IV extends the memory of the dead to include "all the dead whose faith is known to you alone." God's will to save all includes more people than we are able to officially register as members. This is what St. Augustine means when he says: "God has many people whom the Church does not have."

The explicit wish expressed in these prayers commemorating the dead is that they would "find in your presence light, happiness, and peace" (Eucharistic Prayer I; that they would be brought "into the light of your presence" (Eucharistic Prayer II); that they will be received "into your kingdom" (Eucharistic Prayer III). At this point the following comforting text is inserted into Masses for the dead:

"There we hope to share in your glory
when every tear shall be wiped away.
On that day we shall see you, our God, as you are.
We shall become like you
and praise you for ever through Christ our Lord. . . ."

[38] The English rubric is more simply stated: "The priest prays for them briefly with joined hands" (RM, p. 507).—Trans.

Permit us to give a bit of pastoral counsel at this point. Given the close relationship that most people have with their family members, relatives, and friends who have died, the priest is advised to take time before the Mass begins—perhaps while still at home or on the way to the church—to consider whom he will especially remember by name during this particular celebration of the Mass. That could have the positive side effect of disarming the criticism that one hears more and more frequently: "I and my personal life do not seem to exist as far as the Mass is concerned. That is why it leaves me cold and indifferent."

An additional intercession applies to the participants in the Eucharistic celebration. In Eucharistic Prayer II it follows the commemoration of the dead:

"Have mercy on us all;
make us worthy to share eternal life."

Although Eucharistic Prayers III and IV include this petition only in brief and summary form, Eucharistic Prayer I is especially expansive. In this Eucharistic Prayer there is a remembrance of the living that explicitly mentions "all of us gathered here before you." Another follows toward the end of the Canon:

"For ourselves, too, we ask
some share in the fellowship of your apostles and martyrs. . . .
Do not consider what we truly deserve,
but grant us your forgiveness."

This confession of sinfulness and prayer for pardon, a kind of duplication of the penitential act, coming in the context of the praise and thanksgiving of the Eucharistic Prayer, must be considered as not especially successful.

A special kind of intercession arises out of our faith that we stand in fellowship with the saints and that they pray with us and intercede for us, especially when we celebrate Mass. Thus Eucharistic Prayer II commemorates "Mary, the virgin Mother of God, . . . the apostles, and . . . all the saints who have done your will throughout the ages." Eucharistic Prayer IV is similar. In Eucharistic Prayer III the Mother of God, the apostles, the martyrs, and all saints are mentioned, with the option of adding the saint(s) of the day or the patron saint.

The old Roman Canon develops this remembering of the saints far more extensively. This first happens after the remembrance of the living. The first to be named is Mary, the Mother of God. In accordance with an instruction of Pope John XXIII, St. Joseph's name was added in 1962. Then the twelve apostles, the early bishops of Rome and other martyrs, and "all the saints" are included.

A second remembering of the saints appears toward the end of the Canon, following the commemoration of the dead, as part of the above-mentioned prayer *Nobis quoque* ("For ourselves, too"). Here John the Baptist, seven male martyrs, and seven female martyrs are mentioned.

Apart from the names of saints mentioned in the Bible, the people remembered are exclusively men and women who were especially venerated in the ancient congregation of the city of Rome. Most of them mean very little to contemporary congregations, especially since we have only legendary reports of many. So it is understandable that the revisions of the Roman Missal, both in the Latin and in its vernacular editions, place their names in parentheses or brackets. Twenty-one names in the first group of saints and eleven names in the second group are dealt with in this way.

The Concluding Doxology
All the Eucharistic Prayers close with praise of the Trinity in the form of the final doxology. At this point the priest lifts the paten with the hosts and the chalice and says or sings:

"Through him,
with him,
in him,
in the unity of the Holy Spirit,
all glory and honor is yours,
almighty Father,
for ever and ever."

In this doxology we encounter "the classical formula underlying all Christian prayer,"[39] that is, the praise of the Father through Jesus Christ in the Holy Spirit. The whole earthly life of Jesus was a glorification of the Father, as he explicitly states in the high priestly prayer: "I glorified you on earth by finishing the work that you gave me to do" (John 17:4). This work climaxes in his sacrificial offering on the cross, which the Eucharistic Prayer remembers sacramentally. In close communion with him, by the power of our membership in his Mystical Body, we too offer praise and glorification to the Father. This takes place in the Holy Spirit, who is the love that flows back from the Son to the Father.

The congregation reinforces this doxology of praise with the Hebrew word "Amen," meaning, "Yes, that is so." Justin Martyr, an early Christian philosopher, attributed very special meaning to this word when used at the end of the thanksgiving. The great Bible scholar St. Jerome (✝ 420) compares this loud "Amen" spoken by the faithful in the Roman basilicas to thunder from heaven. St. Augustine (✝ 430) describes it as the congregation's signature under the prayer of the priest.

At the end of the Eucharistic Prayer, this "Amen" does not refer merely to the final doxology but rather to the whole Eucharistic Prayer, including the sacrifice of Christ re-presented in this prayer as well as the self-sacrifice of the Church which becomes part of it. Thus it is an important contribution to the prayer on the part of the congregation. For this reason the rubrics of the Missal require that the priest replace the elevated paten and chalice on the altar only after this "Amen."

C. COMMUNION

The remembering of Christ's paschal mystery, together with its sacramental re-presentation and the concomitant self-offering of the Church, is followed by the memorial meal of his body and blood, the Communion. This completes the Eucharistic celebration and our active participation in it. It is an essential part of the

[39] Josef A. Jungmann, *The Mass: An Historical, Theological, and Pastoral Survey*, trans. Julian Fernandes, ed. Mary Ellen Evans (Collegeville, Minn.: The Liturgical Press, 1976), p. 204.

whole celebration, its second high point, indeed its ultimate goal. For the words of institution command us to "take and eat" and to "take and drink" in so prominent a way that we cannot ignore it. Should some wish to stop with "transubstantiation piety" and be satisfied with that, they would only participate in half the celebration of the Eucharist and would not reach the goal set for them by Christ. The meaning and purpose of the Eucharistic celebration is our communion with Christ and with one another.

Having said this makes it clear that broad groups of Christians have, over the course of the history of the Church, deviated from the true view of the Eucharist by being content to receive Communion only once or twice a year or even less frequently. There were already complaints about this practice in the East in the fourth century. The West was not far behind.

The basis for this development was not so much a defective spirituality as it was an exaggerated reverence before the "awful mystery" (*mysterium tremendum*), so that people came to Communion only in fear and trembling. This awe became so strong in the Middle Ages that the Fourth Lateran Council felt it necessary to make it a duty to receive Communion at least once a year. At the cost of the kind of Eucharistic celebration that Christ intended, forms of venerating the elements in solitary, individual piety developed. This situation began to change for the better only as a result of the pastoral-liturgical concerns of Pope Pius X (1903–1914) and the decrees on frequent Communion (1905) and early Communion (1910).

The word "communion" comes from the Latin *communire* and originally referred to a common concern or a common possession. The Church began to use it to describe the fellowship of the Church, from which one could be excommunicated as a result of serious transgression. However, it finally achieved its most important meaning as unity and community with Christ through its use in the sacred meal in the biblical sense of John 6:56: "Those who eat my flesh and drink my blood abide in me, and I in them."

In the oldest descriptions of the Eucharist that we have, the reception of the sanctified gifts followed immediately after the great doxology. However, several preparatory rites developed very early. The first of these was the Our Father.

The Our Father
The Lord's Prayer was used in various liturgies, including the Roman liturgies, as early as the fourth century. Its theological function was interpreted as "both the end of the sacrificial mystery and as preparation for the communion," "as a parenthesis between the sacrificial action and the table fellowship with Christ which it made possible."[40] In the Roman liturgies of the Mass it no longer immediately precedes the reception of communion but rather the rite of peace, the rite of the breaking of the bread, and the rite of commingling. These developments go back to Pope Gregory the Great (590–604).

The Our Father is introduced by an invitation to pray. This invitation reminds us that we cannot take it for granted that we are able, with the faith of children, to address the infinitely great, almighty God as Father. We can only do so because of Jesus' divine instruction. Jesus gave us a new relationship to God and taught us to pray this prayer (see Matt 6:9ff. and Luke 11:1ff.). As a result, we can dare to call God "Father." In addition to the traditional Roman invitation to pray, the Missal adds three other forms of invitation.

The first three petitions of this prayer are related to the content of the preceding Eucharistic Prayer. For here the "name" of God, that is, God's very being, is recognized and praised as holy (for example, in the *Sanctus* and the post-*Sanctus*) and given "all glory and honor" through Christ's sacrifice. Re-presenting the paschal mystery prepares for the commingling of God's kingdom. Through Jesus' obedience to the will of the Father in suffering and death, the highest obedience is demonstrated (see Luke 22:42: "Father, if you are willing, remove this cup from me; yet, not my will but yours be done.")

[40] Walter Dürig, "*Das Vaterunser in der Messe,*" in *Gemeinde im Herrenmahl. Zur Praxis der Messfeier,* 2nd ed., ed. Theodor Mass-Ewerd and Klemens Richter (Freiburg: Herder, 1976), p. 326.

A still more decisive reason for the adoption of the Our Father in the liturgy of the Mass may, however, be found in those two petitions that are especially closely related to the reception of Communion: the petitions asking for bread and for forgiveness.

The petition for daily bread includes everything that we human beings need for life in the fullest sense of the word. This includes food and drink and many other things (for example, a place to work) as the basis for all the possibilities of life and activity. We are depressed by the awareness that this daily bread is the main concern of vast numbers of people. Those who are not worried about bread should pray this petition on behalf of the millions of people who are hungry. At the same time, the early Church fathers drew attention to that bread of which Christ says: "One does not live by bread alone, but by every word that comes from the mouth of God" (Matt 4:4; this is a quotation from Deut 8:3). Finally, in the third century writers such as Tertullian and Cyprian understood this to be the bread of which Jesus says: "The bread that I will give for the life of the world is my flesh" (John 6:51). In this sense the Our Father can be called an Eucharistic table prayer.

The following petition for the forgiveness of guilt was also seen as preparation for receiving Communion. Early Christianity was deeply impressed by Paul's statement about unworthy eating and drinking as the cause of experiencing judgment (1 Cor 11:27ff.). Augustine describes this petition as a necessary washing of our face before we receive Communion. In addition, this petition is combined with the demand that we forgive those who have sinned against us.

As the following rite of peace makes clear, reconciliation with one's brother or sister is a presupposition of worship. Jesus himself requires it in the Sermon on the Mount: "So when you are offering your gift at the altar, if you remember that your brother or sister has something against you, leave your gift there before the altar and go; first be reconciled to your brother or sister, and then come and offer your gift" (Matt 5:23f.). This admonition is repeated in equally insistent form in Matthew 6:14f. Undoubtedly there are many cases in which it is not at all easy to objectively examine our relationships to other people and to create peace through forgiveness and reconciliation. Even so, Christ's word allows no exceptions. At the very least, we must make a serious effort toward reconciliation.

Before the reform of the liturgy, the priest prayed or sang the Our Father by himself. The congregation participated only in the final petition (*sed libera nos a malo*). Already during Vatican II, the first instruction on carrying out the Constitution on the Liturgy, entitled *Inter Oecumenici*, issued on September 26, 1964, cautiously opened the possibility that the Our Father could be prayed or sung by the priest and the congregation together. This was done through an instruction that provides the following options: ''In recited Masses the congregation may recite the Lord's Prayer in the vernacular along with the celebrant; in sung Masses the people may sing it in Latin along with the celebrant and, should the territorial ecclesiastical authority have so decreed, also in the vernacular, using melodies approved by the same authority.''[41] This possibility was quickly utilized with great joy. The Missal provides a melody for singing the Our Father.

In many congregations the Our Father of the Sunday Mass is sung more energetically and with greater inner spirituality than any other song. It seems that the source and the consecrated solemnity of this text motivate congregations to special trust. This trust constitutes the high point of active participation in worship.

The Embolism with Acclamation
The Our Father is followed by a prayer called the ''embolism.'' This is the English version of a Greek word meaning ''insertion.'' Part of the old Roman Order of the Mass, it is also found, with slight textual variations, in all the Eastern liturgies except the Byzantine. It develops the theme of the last petition of the Our Father: ''Save us, almighty Father, from all evil. . . .''

The Latin and German texts of the Our Father leave the question open as to whether the word ''evil'' refers to the personal ''evil

[41] *DOL*, p. 98, no. 48g.

one'' (Satan) or to impersonal ''evil'' such as sin and all troubles. The English embolism clearly defines this term in the second sense by adding ''from every evil'' (Latin: *ab omnibus malis*). After that the priest prays for peace, for God's saving mercy, and for protection against ''all anxiety.''

These concerns are not irrelevant to daily life. ''Peace in our day'' is threatened somewhere or other on the earth every day. Any local conflict can quickly escalate into a worldwide threat to peace. The prayer for protection from sin is equally relevant. To a very large extent, our society is characterized by a terrifying loss of direction and a confusion of concepts, which can far too quickly lead us to turn away from truth and justice, from God and his commandments. The extensive development of our technical means of communication makes it possible for such errors and confusions to spread very rapidly. Therefore these petitions are directly relevant to our present situation. They concern everyone. For ''if you think you are standing, watch out that you do not fall'' (1 Cor 10:12). And Jesus himself warns us in his farewell address: ''Do not let your hearts be troubled'' (John 14:1).

While the reform of the liturgy shortened and tightened the section of the embolism discussed to this point, it expanded it by adding an eschatological closing sentence:

''. . . protect us from all anxiety
as we wait in joyful hope
for the coming of our Savior, Jesus Christ.''

The whole history of salvation will not be complete until Christ returns. The New Testament repeatedly demands that we remain alert and wide awake while waiting for this final Christ-event. This is the basic attitude of Christian life. Referring to the fact that many parishes have arbitrarily omitted this embolism, the liturgical scholar Emil J. Lengeling has commented:

''Any therefore who, exercising their 'own authority' (*SC* 22, 3), deprive the congregation of the embolism thereby thoughtlessly rob these congregations of an important prayer that is 'catholic' in a twofold sense of the term. It is catholic in terms of time, since the Church has spoken this expansion of the Our Father for more than sixteen hundred years. And it is also catholic in a spatial sense, since this prayer is prayed as part of the Church's celebration of the Mass everywhere in the world, in the Masses celebrated by the Western Church as well as in the Eastern Churches, those separated from and those united with Rome."[42]

This eschatological final sentence of the embolism, which is spoken aloud by the priest, is fortunately followed by the congregation's acclamation: "For the kingdom, the power, and the glory are yours, now and for ever." This statement of praise is an "original" prayer of Christianity. It is found already in the *Didache*, or the *Teaching of the Twelve Apostles*, written toward the end of the first century, and is derived from 1 Chronicles 29:11. It has also been adopted in most of the Eastern liturgies. It expresses the early congregations' strong confidence that the kingdom of God would finally triumph, and it has some similarities to the acclamations glorifying God that are found in the Book of Revelation (e.g., 5:12; 19:1). The conclusion of the *Gloria* praises Christ in a parallel way:

"For you alone are the Holy One,
you alone are the Lord,
you alone are the Most High. . . ."

The old Roman Missal did not contain this statement of praise. By including it in the present Roman Missal, the liturgical reform succeeded in recapturing a primitive Christian prayer. At the same time, a small step in the direction of ecumenical unity has also been taken. For the Churches of the Reformation always add this prayer to the Our Father, ever since Martin Luther, following the example of the Greek text of the New Testament he was using, included it in his translation of the Bible.

The Rite of Peace
The prayers and gestures of this rite are also a direct preparation for receiving Communion. In the Sermon on the Mount, Jesus em-

---

[42] *Gottesdienst* 13 (1979), p. 70.

phatically requires that reconciliation with one's brother or sister must take place before worship (see Matt 5:23f.). For this reason it is also understandable that the rite of peace appears in the Eastern liturgies after the service of the Word and the intercessions. This was also originally the case in the West, until Pope Gregory the Great moved it to its present place.

We distinguish three parts of the rite of peace: (a) the prayer for peace, together with the preceding invitation to pray; (b) the priest's wish of peace for the congregation; and (c) the sign of peace.

a) The priest's invitation to pray before the prayer of peace is based on John 14:27:

"Lord Jesus Christ, you said to your apostles:
I leave you peace, my peace I give you."

Here we should remember that the word "peace" as used by Christ means more than the absence of war and conflict. He used the Hebrew-Aramaic term "Shalom," which was used by the prophets as a term comprehending all messianic salvation. It includes all well-being, both of body and of soul. That also requires complete harmony between the individual and God and among people. This great gift of God is the fruit of the paschal mystery, the fullness of the salvation of the new covenant.

The prayer for peace itself is not addressed to the Father but rather to Christ:

"Look not on our sins, but on the faith of your Church,
and grant us the peace and unity of your kingdom."

b) The wish of peace for the congregation comes after this prayer of peace. The priest extends his hands and says: "The peace of the Lord be with you always." The congregation answers: "And also with you."

The extending of the hands at this place was "originally a kind of collective embrace; as such, it differs from the similar gesture made during the invitation prayer ('Let us pray') and from the orant posture which the celebrant adopts during his presidential prayers."[43]

c) According to ancient usage, the wish for peace may be followed by a visible sign of peace. The priest or the deacon may invite the congregation to "make an appropriate sign of peace, according to local custom" by saying, "Let us offer each other the sign of peace."

The details of the way in which this visible sign of peace is given (for example, by a kiss, a handshake, or by a bow) is to be determined by the conference of bishops in accordance with the particular culture and customs of the people. This most often takes the form of a handshake. The priest himself gives the sign of peace to those who are assisting at the altar.

The Rite of Breaking of the Bread
After the rite of peace the priest breaks the large host into several pieces. Such a multiplying of the number of pieces used to be a practical necessity, insofar as the usual large, flat pieces of bread had to be broken into small pieces so that they could be distributed to the faithful. As all the institution narratives prove, this is what Jesus did at the Last Supper. He took the bread, spoke the prayer of thanks, broke the bread, and gave it to the disciples. The early Church itself saw this process as having deep symbolism. Thus Paul writes: "The bread that we break, is it not a sharing in the body of Christ? Because there is one bread, we who are many are one body, for we all partake of the one bread" (1 Cor 10:16f.).

This interpretation reveals that the Eucharistic bread symbolizes Christians' unity with Christ and with one another. The General Instruction therefore stands on the basis of the most ancient and unbroken tradition when it writes:

"The action of the breaking of the bread, the simple term for the eucharist in apostolic times, will more clearly bring out the force

[43] Johannes H. Emminghaus, *The Eucharist: Essence, Form, Celebration*, p. 193.

and meaning of the sign of the unity of all in the one bread and of their charity, since the one bread is being distributed among the members of one family" (*GIRM* 283; cf. *GIRM* 56c).

In the twelfth century the pre-formed host, about as large as a coin, came into use. As a result, the breaking of the bread was no longer practiced. The priest only broke the larger host into three unequal parts and dropped the smallest piece into the chalice (see below, p. 104). He consumed both of the larger pieces in his own Communion. Thus the deep symbolism of the breaking of the bread was completely lost. The reform of the Mass under Pope Paul VI attempted to restore it by having the priest break one or more large hosts into small pieces and distribute them to at least a few of the faithful (*GIRM* 283). This should be done especially when the Mass is concelebrated or celebrated for smaller groups, as well as for wedding Masses and for confirmation; then at least the newly confirmed should receive pieces of the broken hosts.

The new Missal is attempting to introduce a development that will not be immediately accepted. For this reason the General Instruction (*GIRM* 283) provides: "When, however, the number of communicants is large or other pastoral needs require it, small hosts are in no way ruled out." This concession, however, should not be understood as a license permitting "a practice that is only intended to make things easier and to get things over sooner by permitting a quicker, easier, and less complicated celebration."[44] Rather, the task is find ways of breaking the bread during the Mass itself and to distribute its pieces to all the communicants, even in large congregations. Perhaps this could be done by preparing larger pieces of bread scored for breaking. To do this, it would be necessary to use a kind of bread that does not easily crumble.

It is not just recently that the Church has placed great value on all the communicants' receiving only hosts that have been consecrated in that particular celebration of the Mass. The explicit

[44] Franz Nikolasch, "Vom geteilten Brot," in Josef C. Plöger, ed., *Gott feiern. Theologische Anregung und geistliche Vertiefung zur Feier von Messe und Stundengebet* (Freiburg: Herder, 1980), p. 249.

wish that this would happen was expressed by Vatican II's Constitution on the Liturgy (*SC* 55), the General Instruction (*GIRM* 56h), and in other postconciliar documents. Before that, it was the wish of Pius XII,[45] who cites Benedict XIV (1740–1758) as an authority. The original purpose of storing consecrated hosts in the tabernacle was to have them available at all times for Viaticum to the critically ill. It is as surprising as it is deplorable that many parishes simply ignore this meaningful recommendation of several popes and continue to consecrate in order to "stock up ahead of time."[46]

The Rite of Commingling

The dropping of part of the host into the chalice (commingling) while speaking the prayer "May this mingling of the body and blood of our Lord Jesus Christ bring eternal life to us who receive it" is not easy to explain. The General Instruction does not attempt any explanation of this rite. In the opinion of many scholars, it is derived from an old Roman custom. The pope sent a piece of the consecrated host (called the *fermentum*) to the priests of neighboring churches. Bishops of other cities did something similar. The priests placed this piece of the host in the chalice during the next celebration of the Mass. This was a sign of brotherhood with the pope (or the bishop) and a symbol of the oneness of Christ's sacrifice. Other scholars see this rite as an adoption of a rite developed in Syria. This rite symbolized the resurrection of Christ and his presence on the altar. We can forgo the attempt to add additional explanations.

In view of hypotheses of this kind, some historical, some allegorical, it is proper to ask why this rite was not eliminated in the reform of the Mass. This question is justified because Vatican II specifically directed: "The rites should be distinguished by a noble simplicity. They should be short, clear, and free from useless repetitions. They should be within the people's powers of comprehension, and normally should not require much explanation" (*SC* 34). Speaking specifically of the rites of the Mass, it says: "The rites

[45] *Mediator Dei*, 119 and 121.
[46] Emil J. Lengeling, *Die neue Ordnung der Eucharistiefeier*, p. 246.

are to be simplified, due care being taken to preserve their substance. Parts which with the passage of time came to be duplicated, or were added with little advantage, are to be omitted" (*SC* 50).

In spite of this, however, the decision of those responsible was not made merely out of consideration for conservative groups but rather primarily because of the fact that most of the Eastern liturgies perform this rite as a very solemn ceremony. For the purposes of explaining it in catechetical instruction and in homilies, we might agree that it is to be understood as a symbol of the presence of the exalted Christ. Indeed, he does not meet us in the Eucharist as the dead Christ on the cross, whose body and blood are separated, but rather as the risen Lord.

The Agnus Dei

"During the breaking of the bread and the commingling, the *Agnus Dei* is as a rule sung by the choir or cantor with the congregation responding; otherwise it is recited aloud. This invocation may be repeated as often as necessary to accompany the breaking of the bread. The final reprise concludes with the words, *grant us peace*" (*GIRM* 56e).

This invocation of Christ was first introduced into the Roman celebration of the Mass by Pope Sergius I (687–701). It was intended to accompany the breaking of the bread, a rite that then required more time. Since the eleventh century the last invocation has concluded with "grant us peace" rather than "have mercy on us."

The designation of Christ as the "Lamb of God" is found already in the New Testament. It occurs as a title used by John the Baptist (John 1:29, 36) and appears especially often in the Book of Revelation (e.g., 5:6ff.; 19:9). This usage is based on Isaiah 53:7: "Like a lamb that is led to the slaughter . . . so he did not open his mouth." Thus this invocation of Christ is a clear reference to his sacrificial death. Paul also compares Christ to the Passover lamb: "For our paschal lamb, Christ, has been sacrificed" (1 Cor 5:7).

Thus this chant of the congregation is a song in praise of Christ who sacrificed himself for us and who is present on the altar as the exalted Lord with his sacrificial surrender. He has the divine power to grant us mercy and peace.

Prayer of Preparation and Invitation
When the rite of the breaking of the bread and its accompanying song are finished, the priest prays two prayers of preparation inaudibly. One can immediately recognize that they are not part of the old Roman liturgy from the fact that they use the first person singular pronouns "I" and "me," and are addressed, not to the Father, but rather to Christ. Both are taken from the Gaulish-Frankish liturgy of the ninth or tenth century. The first remembers Christ's redeeming death and attaches various petitions. The second, in its present form much shorter than previously, starts with a reference to Paul's warning against an unworthy reception of Communion (1 Cor 11:27-29). The faithful join in this preparation through their own silent prayers (*GIRM* 56f). In this connection it should be noted that the preceding rites and prayers are also real preparation.

After a genuflection, a custom that was still unknown at this point even in the late Middle Ages, the priest raises a piece of the broken host over the paten and makes a statement based on John 1:29:

"This is the Lamb of God
who takes away the sins of the world.
Happy are those who are called to his supper."

The last line, a quotation from Revelation 19:9, refers to the eschatological fulfillment, for which the reception of Communion is a guarantee, on the basis of Christ's promise (see John 6:51, 54).

Next the priest and the congregation together speak the words of the centurion of Capernaum (Matt 8:8). These words express humility and great trust:

"Lord, I am not worthy to receive you,
but only say the word and I shall be healed."

The Priest's Communion

The priest is the first to take the host and to drink out of the chalice. Before receiving Communion, he prays: "May the body (blood) of Christ bring me to everlasting life." However, if there are concelebrants, a deacon, or ministers of the Eucharist at the altar, he first gives the sacred bread to them, and they then all receive it at the same time.

In our time the rule of the Missal requiring the priest to receive Communion first has sometimes evoked vehement controversy. One author puts it this way: "The rule that the priest should commune before the congregation is an unhappy decision. A good host does not do that. For this reason many priests immediately begin to distribute to the congregation and receive Communion at the end. Then no one needs to wait for them. . . ."[47] The demand for this change is contradicted by both historical and ecumenical considerations, but especially by theological concerns.

Since the beginning it has been the consistent practice of all liturgies of the East and the West that the celebrating bishop or priest is the first to take Communion. Any attempt to change this order would encounter significant opposition, especially from the Eastern Churches. It would be condemned as a deviation from the traditional order. Theological tradition makes it very clear that the precedence given to the priest is not to be regarded as a privilege of rank or pride of hierarchical position, but rather is particularly appropriate to his office as the leader of the congregation and as the "servant of all" (Mark 9:35). We ought not equate the Eucharistic meal with an ordinary banquet and make those table customs the pattern for the Eucharist.

The true meaning of the Communion is, as we have explained, the completion of our participation in Christ's sacrifice: We are graciously incorporated into his offering of himself to the Father. The communicants participate by offering their own selves. The host and master of the feast is not the priest but rather Christ.

[47] Winfried Blasig, *Für einen menschengerechten Gottesdienst: Anregungen zur liturgischen Praxis und zur Fortführung der Liturgiereform* (Munich: Kösel, 1981), p. 76.

Thus the priest's precedence in communing expresses the fact that he is the first to accept Christ's invitation to be ready to offer himself and that he leads the congregation by his example.

There is, however, a reply that can be given to those who still wish to change this order of communing on the basis of supposedly polite table manners. This is admittedly an *ad hominem* argument, that is, not really germane to the issue, but perhaps an effective reply: Even at a secular banquet the guests would be considered to have violated commonly accepted rules of politeness if they were to start eating and drinking before the host did.

The Communion of the Faithful

During the Communion of the faithful, the Communion song is sung. This song should already begin when the priest receives. "Its function is to express outwardly the communicants' union in spirit by means of the unity of their voices, to give evidence of joy of heart, and to make the procession to receive Christ's body more fully an act of community" (*GIRM* 56i).

Different possible choices for this song are described in more detail: "An antiphon from the *Graduale Romanum* may also be used, with or without the psalm, or an antiphon with psalm from *The Simple Gradual* or another suitable song approved by the conference of bishops. It is sung by the choir alone or by the choir or cantor with the congregation" (*GIRM* 56i). If the Communion song is not sung, "the communion antiphon in the Missal is recited either by the people, by some of them, or by a reader. Otherwise the priest himself says it after he has received communion and before he gives communion to the faithful" (*GIRM* 56i).

When distributing Communion, the priest (deacon, acolyte, or Eucharistic minister) shows the host to each communicant by elevating it slightly and saying "The body of Christ." The communicant answers "Amen." This distribution formula is first recorded by the Doctor of the Church St. Ambrose of Milan (✝ 397). It is basically shorter and more practical to use with a large number of communicants than the earlier formula: "May the body of our Lord Jesus Christ preserve your soul to eternal life." Brief though it is, it contains the essential Eucharistic confession of faith. It expresses Christ's own words of institution, "This is my body."

When the faithful speak their "Amen," they affirm their faith in the presence of the Lord who offers himself for us. They also affirm their inner readiness to join in this offering. The "Amen" should therefore be spoken clearly and audibly rather than murmured. Of course, each individual should take the presence of other participants into consideration when responding.

Because of the various floor plans of the individual churches, no universal rule can be stated regarding the place at which Communion is distributed.

Receiving Communion in the Hand or on the Tongue?
Until sometime in the ninth century, it was the general custom to place the host, the gift of the holy God, in the hand of the communicant. A vivid example of this custom and of deep reverence for the body of the Lord is found in the *Mystagogical Catecheses* (V, 21f.) of St. Cyril of Jerusalem late in the fourth century:

"Coming up to receive, therefore, . . . making your left hand a throne for the right (for it is about to receive a King) . . . and cupping your palm, so receive the Body of Christ; and answer: 'Amen.' Carefully hallow your eyes by the touch of the sacred Body, and then partake, taking care to lose no part of it. . . . guard against losing so much as a crumb of that which is more precious than gold or precious stones!"[48]

Sometime later, people were expected to receive the host with a hand covered by a white linen cloth. In the ninth century, as

[48] *The Works of Saint Cyril of Jerusalem,* trans. Leo P. McCauley and Anthony A. Stephenson (Washington: Catholic University of America Press, 1970), vol. 2, p. 203. Volume 64 of *The Fathers of the Church. A New Translation,* ed. Bernard M. Peebles et al. The *Mystagogical Catecheses* were addressed to the newly baptized. These catecheses are ordinarily attributed to St. Cyril of Jerusalem but may also have been prepared by his successor John.

reverence and holy awe of the host continued to increase, the host was placed directly on the tongue of the communicant. People believed that this was the best way to avoid the danger of small crumbs falling to the floor or of the host being misused for some other purposes.

After Vatican II, efforts to permit Communion in the hand intensified in many countries. The Pope surveyed the conferences of bishops, and most of them spoke in favor of the exclusive practice of receiving Communion on the tongue. However, out of consideration for the significant minority, the Sacred Congregation for Divine Worship issued an instruction permitting the conferences of bishops in those territories in which the custom of receiving Communion with the hand was already widely practiced to decide to allow it by a two-thirds secret vote, subject to approval by the Apostolic See.[49]

The conferences of bishops in German-speaking lands as well as others made use of this possibility already in 1969 and promulgated corresponding regulations. They emphasized that the host cannot be self-administered from bowls, whether these are set out in a specific place or passed from hand to hand. To the contrary, the person distributing Communion should place the host into the hand of individual communicants, and the communicants should immediately place it into their mouths (distribution instead of "self-service"). Apart from this, it does not matter in which hand the host is placed.

Both forms of receiving Communion can and must be combined with the proper reverence, which is fueled by faith. Even though the anxious awe as well as the exaggerated consciousness of sin and unworthiness that were common in many past centuries are not to be considered as ideal, neither is the opposite attitude of irreverence. Non-Christians who are present at the celebration of the Mass must recognize that they are in the presence of a deep mystery of faith.

[49] Instruction *Memoriale Domini*, on the manner of giving Communion. May 29, 1969. *DOL*, pp. 643ff., at 646.

Communion from the Chalice by the Faithful

In all the institution narratives as well as in the Eucharistic promises (John 6), drinking from the sacred chalice is equally as important as eating the transformed bread. We are therefore not surprised that Communion from the chalice by the laity was, at first, the common practice of all Christian Churches. This was also the practice in the Roman Catholic Church until the thirteenth century. Its slow disappearance probably had two causes: the exaggerated and anxious concern that great wrong would be committed if the holy blood of Christ were spilled; and the understanding of medieval theology that the whole, living Christ, together with his blood, is present in the transformed bread. This is the doctrine of "concomitance." The sharing of the chalice by the laity was first officially forbidden at the Council of Constance in 1415. This was done in reaction to the Hussite teaching that receiving Communion under both kinds is necessary to salvation. When the Reformation also adopted this teaching, the rejection of Communion from the chalice became really intense.

The first cautious approach to the original custom took place at Vatican II. The Constitution on the Liturgy says:

"The dogmatic principles which were laid down by the Council of Trent remaining intact, communion under both kinds may be granted when the bishops think fit, not only to clerics and religious but also to the laity, in cases to be determined by the Holy See" (*SC* 55).

After this, this possibility was broadened, with the result that the General Instruction already lists fourteen groups of persons who are allowed to share in the chalice (*GIRM* 242). A further extension was made by the instruction *Sacramentali Communione* of June 29, 1970, which gave conferences of bishops even greater authority to extend this practice.[50] The American bishops responded by authorizing Communion from the chalice at weekday Masses and at Masses for other special occasions. On October 13, 1984, the

---

[50] Sacred Congregation for Divine Worship, instruction *Sacramentali Communione*, extending Communion under both kinds. *DOL*, pp. 664ff.

Congregation for Divine Worship confirmed a decree of the National Conference of Catholic Bishops allowing Communion under both kinds at Masses on Sundays and holydays of obligation if done in an "orderly and reverent" manner.[51]

The basis for this reduction of a centuries-long reluctance to receive Communion is described in the General Instruction:

"Holy Communion has a more complete form as a sign when it is received under both kinds. For in this manner of reception a fuller light shines on the sign of the Eucharistic banquet. Moreover there is a clearer expression of that will by which the new and everlasting covenant is ratified in the blood of the Lord and of the relationship of the eucharistic banquet to the eschatological banquet in the Father's kingdom" (*GIRM* 240).

In each individual case the celebrating priest or, in parish churches, the pastor, shall decide if these far-reaching possibilities are to be used.

The General Instruction recognizes four possible forms and ways of Communion from the chalice:

    a) drinking from the chalice;
    b) intinction of the host in the chalice;
    c) use of a drinking tube;
    d) use of a small spoon, with which small particles of host that have been dipped into the chalice are administered to the mouth (*GIRM* 243–252).

The instruction on Communion under both kinds (*Sacramentali Communione*) recognizes that drinking directly from the chalice is preferred because it is the fullest symbol. The minister, before he administers the chalice, speaks the words "The blood of Christ," and the communicant answers "Amen." Ordinarily the communi-

---

[51] See *GIRM*, Appendix, no. 242. On all that pertains to receiving Communion under both kinds, see the National Conference of Catholic Bishops, *This Holy and Living Sacrifice: Directory for the Celebration and Reception of Communion under Both Kinds*, which contains the rules for the United States.

cants take the chalice in their hands, drink from it, and then hand it back to the minister, who each time then cleanses the rim of the chalice with a small cloth. In Masses in which Communion under both kinds is distributed, individual believers are free to choose whether they wish to drink from the chalice or not.

During the first Christian millennium it was usual, both in the East and in the West, to receive Communion while standing. This custom was especially suggested by receiving the chalice. During the twelfth century the custom of receiving while kneeling began to be practiced. Following Vatican II, the custom of receiving Communion while standing was reintroduced. The instruction on worship of the Eucharist gives communicants the choice of receiving Communion while kneeling or while standing.[52] At the same time it recommends that various circumstances, especially space limitations and the number of communicants, should be taken into account and that communicants should willingly conform to the method announced by the pastors so that the Communion will remain a sign of brotherly unity.

Receiving Communion Twice on the Same Day
According to a centuries-old custom that has also been ratified by canon law, Communion should be received only once a day. However, the instruction on the worship of the Eucharist provides for three cases in which the faithful are permitted to receive a second time:

a) When a Mass is celebrated on Saturday evening or on the evening before a holy day of obligation in which the faithful wish to fulfill their Sunday obligation, even though they already received Communion in the morning;

b) In a Mass celebrated on Easter Sunday or on Christmas Day, even though they have already received communion during the Mass of the Easter Vigil or during the Mass of the Lord's Nativity (Midnight Mass);

[52] Sacred Congregation of Rites, *Eucharisticum Mysterium*, on worship of the Eucharist, May 25, 1967. *DOL*, p. 410, no. 34a.

113

c) In the Mass on Holy Thursday evening, even though they have already received communion in the Chrism Mass.[53]

This permission was then significantly expanded by the Congregation for the Discipline of the Sacraments on January 29, 1973:[54]

"There may however be special circumstances in which the faithful who have already received communion on the same day or in which priests who have celebrated Mass attend some community's celebration. It will be lawful for these faithful and these priests to receive communion a second time in the following situations:

1. at ritual Masses in which the sacraments of baptism, confirmation, anointing of the sick, orders, and marriage are administered, as well as at Masses in which there is a first communion;

2. at Masses for the consecration of a church or an altar, for a religious profession, for the conferral of a "canonical mission";

3. at the Masses for the dead on the occasion of the funeral, news of the death, the final burial, or the first anniversary;

4. at the principal Mass celebrated in a cathedral or parish church on the solemnity of Corpus Christi and on the day of a pastoral visitation; at a Mass celebrated on the occasion of a major religious superior's canonical visitation to a particular religious house or chapter;

5. at the principal Mass at a eucharistic or Marian congress, whether international or national, regional or diocesan;

6. at the principal Mass of any kind of meeting, pilgrimage, or people's mission;

7. at the administration of viaticum, when communion may be given to the members of the household and the friends of the sick person who are present.

8. Over and above the cases already mentioned, the local Ordinary is allowed to grant for a single occasion the faculty to receive communion twice on the same day whenever, because of truly

[53] Ibid., p. 407, no. 28.
[54] Congregation for the Discipline of the Sacraments, *Immensae Caritatis*, on facilitating reception of Communion in certain circumstances, January 29, 1973. *DOL*, pp. 652–653.

special circumstances, a second reception is warranted on the basis of this Instruction.''

The Eucharistic Fast
Early Christians already were familiar with the custom of receiving Communion "before any other food" (Tertullian). The Eastern Churches still preserve the custom of fasting—usually an extended fast—before receiving Communion. The Roman Catholic Church in the late Middle Ages established the rule that no food or drink was to be consumed after midnight when people wished to receive Communion the next morning.

Until World War II, this rule was often overemphasized in catechetical instruction (for example, preparation for first Communion). Not observing this fast was considered to result in an unworthy Communion. During the war, with its numerous air-raid alerts and nights spent without sleep in bomb shelters, this rule was relaxed in various ways required by the difficult living conditions. The following rule is the one that is presently in force; it has been stated in various postconciliar documents:

Healthy people should not consume any food or drink, except for water, during the hour preceding their reception of Communion. However, for certain people the Eucharistic fast has been shortened to some fifteen minutes. We cite the corresponding text according to the instruction *Immensae Caritatis* of January 29, 1973:

1. the sick in health-care facilities or at home, even if they are not bedridden;
2. the faithful of advanced years, whether they are confined to their homes because of old age or live in homes for the aged;
3. sick priests, even if not bedridden, and elderly priests, as regards both celebrating Mass and receiving communion;
4. persons caring for, as well as the family and friends of, the sick and elderly who wish to receive communion with them, whenever such persons cannot keep the one-hour fast without inconvenience.[55]

[55] Ibid., p. 653.

The instruction elaborates on this major reduction of the fast as follows: "To give recognition to the dignity of the sacrament and to stir up joy at the coming of the Lord, it is well to observe a period of silence and recollection."[56]

The rule that provides that anyone in danger of death may receive Viaticum without observing any fast remains valid. This provision was already made in the old Code of Canon Law (can. 858, §1). The new Code of Canon Law (can. 919, §3) appears to reduce the period of fasting for the four groups named above even further. It states that these people are permitted to receive Communion even when they have consumed something during the previous hour.

Ministers of Communion
In the early Church it was a common custom to distribute the Eucharistic bread to the faithful so that they could receive it at home on days when Communion was not celebrated or could take it to the sick and imprisoned. In later centuries laypersons were repeatedly authorized, in emergency situations, to bring Communion to the sick and imprisoned.

After Vatican II the acute shortage of priests in many countries led to a gradually expanding process of commissioning "extraordinary ministers of Holy Communion" ("special ministers of the Eucharist"). Since 1969 women have been eligible for this work. The instruction *Immensae Caritatis* of January 29, 1973, resulted in the final consolidation of this process. It provides for the local ordinary to give permission to suitable laypersons to distribute Communion. This permission may be given for individual cases, for a limited period of time or permanently. It presupposes that no priest, deacon, or acolyte is available for this work or that the number of communicants is so great that the celebration of Mass would last too long. This authority also includes the right to take Communion to the sick, even when it is Viaticum, and to give themselves Communion.

Since 1976 Communion ministers also have the right to lead services of the Word that include the distribution of Communion and

56 Ibid.

to place the Blessed Sacrament in the pyx or monstrance on the altar so that it may be venerated. Benediction with the Blessed Sacrament, however, is reserved to priests and deacons.

The commissioning of such extraordinary ministers of Holy Communion, for which a special rite is provided,[57] is to be announced to the congregations. "No one is to be chosen whose appointment the faithful might find disquieting."[58] In unusual emergency situations the celebrating priest himself may appoint a suitable person to distribute Communion.

Since this policy was established, many thousands of men and women have participated in this ministry. As Günter Duffrer says, we may properly speak of a "successful experiment" that has served the welfare of the congregations.[59] Their commissioning also makes it clear that what we say about the common priesthood of the laity because of their baptism and confirmation is no mere empty word.

The commissioning of ministers of Communion should be preceded by an appropriate course of preparation at the regional or diocesan level. Such preparation not only provides practical guidelines but also includes the theology of the sacrament and the common priesthood. In addition, many dioceses also offer retreat days in which continuing theological education and guidance for developing a deeper spiritual life are offered.

The Cleansing of the Vessels
When the distribution of Communion is finished, the remaining hosts are taken to the tabernacle. However, if there are only a few, they may be consumed by the ministers. This also applies to the remaining consecrated wine when there is Communion from the cup. First, however, the paten is cleansed of any particles of

[57] "Order for the Commissioning of Extraordinary Ministers of Holy Communion" (*Rites*, vol. 2, pp. 142-154) is taken from the *Rite of Commissioning Special Ministers of Holy Communion* (ICEL, 1978).
[58] *Immensae Caritatis* (DOL, p. 652).
[59] Günter Duffrer, "*Ein geglücktes Experiment*," in *Gottesdienst* 7 (1973), pp. 137-140.

host that may remain on it by wiping it with the cloth used to cleanse the rim of the chalice and letting such pieces fall into the wine. Then the chalice is cleansed using wine and water or water alone. The priest (or deacon) drinks this mixture and dries the chalice with the purificator. This cleansing or purification should take place at the side of the altar or at the credence table. While doing this, the priest silently speaks a prayer found in the oldest sacramentaries and referring to the Communion that has been received:

"Lord, may I receive these gifts in purity of heart.
May they bring me healing and strength, now and for ever."

It is also possible to purify the vessels after the Mass, especially when there are several (*GIRM* 120). Undoubtedly such detailed instructions may seem petty to some; however, they express our great reverence for the sacrament and for Christ who is present in it.

Silent Prayer, Song of Thanks, and Closing Prayer
After the distribution of Communion, that is, after the cleansing of the vessels, "the priest and people may spend some time in silent prayer. If desired, a hymn, psalm, or other song of praise may be sung by the entire congregation" (*GIRM* 56j). Such a time of meditation and thanksgiving is wholly appropriate to the meaning of the mystery that has just been received. However, it is advisable to explain occasionally the meaning of this period of silence for prayer so that the people do not become impatient with what may seem to be an unnecessary lengthening of the celebration of the Mass.

The Communion rite, and therewith also the celebration of the Eucharist in the narrower sense, ends with the "prayer after Communion" (Latin: *postcommunio*). It is spoken audibly, as are all the presidential orations, and begins with an invitation to pray spoken by the priest, with outstretched hands, and with the congregation responding "Amen." The priest may stand either at the celebrant's chair or at the altar. The prayer gives thanks for the gift that has been received and combines this thanksgiving with the petition that the mystery just celebrated may continue to bear fruit in this life and in the eternal consummation.

D. CONCLUDING RITES

Pastoral Announcements

After the closing prayer parish announcements or pastoral instructions may be given. This is certainly a better place to do this than the earlier custom of doing so before or after the homily. It would, however, be psychologically wrong to make extensive announcements that could obliterate the remaining impression of the celebration of the Eucharist. Many announcements are more effectively communicated through the parish bulletin or bulletin board. This is true even though the priest "may also make comments concluding the entire sacred service before the dismissal" (*GIRM* 11) and may also include a personal farewell. The priest should stand at the celebrant's chair for these announcements. However, it is recommended that the priest stand at the altar for the following blessing.

The Blessing

It is liturgical custom that the priest proclaims the biblical blessing "The Lord be with you" to the assembly with his hands extended. The congregation responds, "And also with you." The usual words of the blessing, which may be either sung or said while the priest makes the sign of the cross over the congregation, are:

"May almighty God bless you,
the Father, and the Son, and the Holy Spirit."

The congregation affirms this blessing by responding "Amen."

"On certain days or occasions another more solemn form of blessing or prayer over the people may be used" (*RM*, p. 526). When the more solemn form of the blessing is used, the deacon or the priest instructs the people to bow their heads. Then the priest sings or speaks a three-part prayer while extending his hands over the congregation. This concludes with the prayer for blessing:

"May almighty God bless you, the Father, and the Son, and the Holy Spirit."[60]

In the Roman Missal the section entitled "Prayers over the People" opens with the instruction "Bow your heads and pray for God's blessing." This is followed by twenty-six prayers of blessing, which close with the blessing: "May almighty God bless you, the Father, and the Son, and the Holy Spirit."[61] The congregation affirms this prayer by responding "Amen." Such prayers of blessing over the people were previously restricted to weekday masses during Lent. Now, however, they may be used during the whole year, "at the end of Mass, or after the liturgy of the word, the office, and the celebration of the sacraments" (RM, p. 537).

Dismissal of the Congregation
The concluding summons in the Latin Missal is *Ite, missa est*. This is spoken by the deacon or the priest. It literally means, "Go, you are dismissed" (The Latin *missa* is derived from *dimissio*). These words were used already among heathen Greeks and Romans to close an assembly. The English addition "Go in peace" is therefore to be understood as an interpretation that adds meaning to the original. In the Eastern Liturgy of St. John Chrysostom, the dismissal formulas are significantly longer but begin with the priest's summons: "Let us go in peace," to which the congregation responds: "In the name of the Lord."

The word "Mass" comes from this Latin term for dismissal. Since the dismissal very early was combined with the blessing, the word *missa* was understood as referring to the blessing given to participants in the Eucharistic celebration. Another meaning that was suggested for *Ite, missa est* is: "Go, your mission now begins." This derives the meaning of the Latin *missa est* from the similar word *missio* ("mission"). This interpretation was based on the fact that every gift of God also brings us a new task, and the Eucharist obligates us to live thankful lives and to spread the good news of God's grace.

[60] For the texts of the solemn blessings in English, see RM, pp. 528–536.
[61] See RM, pp. 537–540.

This expansion of the original meaning also is directly related to the meaning of the Eucharistic sacrament. Since God's gifts are always intended to be used in service of the kingdom of God, they carry with them the task of spreading that peace which comprehends all divine grace (see above, p. 101). There is a well-known song in German that expresses this obligation very clearly. It describes it in terms of our effort to achieve loving unity of Christians in Christ and to always be ready to bear witness to God's "friendliness" in our conversation and in our lives:

"O Herr, verleih, dass Lieb und Treu
in dir uns all verbinden,
dass Hand und Mund zu jeder Stund
dein Freundlichkeit verkünden,
bis nach der Zeit den Platz bereit
an deinem Tisch wir finden."[62]

"O Lord, grant us that love and faith
may join us all in you,
that hand and mouth in every hour
your friendliness proclaim,
until when life is past,
we all find our place at your heavenly table."

The General Instruction expresses similar thoughts when it describes the concluding rites as sending "each member back to doing good works, while praising and blessing the Lord" (GIRM 57b).

The congregation speaks the final word in the celebration of the Mass: "Thanks be to God." This is a thankful look back at the Eucharistic celebration that is itself a great thanksgiving for a great work of salvation.

Kissing of the Altar and Departure
In leaving, the priest kisses the altar as the symbol of Christ, just as he did as a greeting at the beginning. Together with the

---

[62] This is a stanza of a well-known German song: "Im Frieden dein," in *Gotteslob*, no. 473.

ministers, he bows before the altar and then returns to the sacristy. However, if there is a tabernacle containing the Blessed Sacrament in the sanctuary, they follow the old Roman Catholic custom of genuflecting, as the General Instruction explicitly notes: "If there is a tabernacle with the blessed sacrament in the sanctuary, a genuflection is made before and after Mass and whenever anyone passes in front of the blessed sacrament" (*GIRM* 233). If another liturgical service, for example, a procession, follows the Mass, the concluding rites (greeting, blessing, and dismissal) are omitted (*GIRM* 126).

The practice of singing a closing song varies from parish to parish. Some see the dismissal "Go in peace" as the absolute end of the celebration of the Eucharist, forbidding any further activity. Others sing a song while the priest is leaving. This song is intended to provide a joyful echo either of the Eucharistic celebration or of the current liturgical season. Elsewhere people prefer a musical ending provided by the organ or other musical instruments. A good case can be made for each of these positions, and no general rule can be established. At this point each individual parish may decide how to do this. To quote the famous statement of St. Augustine: "In what is necessary, unity; in cases of uncertainty, freedom; but in every case, love."

Chapter Three

Special Forms of the Celebration of the Mass

The preceding description of the Eucharistic celebration was written with the celebration of Mass with a congregation in mind. We may describe this as the normal form. Alongside this are other styles that are referred to as special forms of the Mass. These include concelebrated Masses, conventual Masses (that is, Masses celebrated in religious communities in conjunction with the Liturgy of the Hours), celebrations of the Mass without a congregation, and finally, those three forms to which we shall pay especially close attention: Mass with children, Mass with young people, and Mass celebrated with small groups.

Vatican II already clearly saw that there can be no ideal form of liturgical celebration. The Constitution on the Sacred Liturgy announces:

"Provided that the substantial unity of the Roman rite is preserved, provision shall be made, when revising the liturgical books, for legitimate variations and adaptations to different groups, regions and peoples, especially in mission countries.

This should be borne in mind when drawing up the rites and determining rubrics" (SC 38).

Here the wise advice of the Danish theologian and author Sören Kierkegaard was taken seriously. His observation has become a pedagogical principle: "If we are to have any success in leading people to a particular place, we must, before anything else, find them where they are and begin at that point."[1]

---

[1] *Die Schriften über sich selbst*, in *Gesammelte Schriften*, vol. 33, p. 38.

In conformity with these basic insights and instructions, the new Missal gives the conferences of bishops authority in their own territories to establish norms "that are suited to the traditions and character of peoples, regions, and various communities" (*GIRM* 6).

MASSES WITH CHILDREN

Such accommodation seemed especially necessary in Masses with children. The conference of bishops of the German-speaking territories provided for the publication of norms and suggestions for worship with children in 1972.[2] This publication was valuable preparation for the *Directory for Masses with Children (DMC)*, which was issued by the Congregation for Divine Worship in Rome on November 1, 1973.[3]

While both of the documents just referred to always preserve the basic structure of the Mass, they also propose a definite simplification. Such simplification is needed to enable children both to understand and actively participate in the Mass as well as to create the conditions necessary for their active participation in the celebration of Mass in the parish. It is important to provide for as active participation of children in the Mass as possible, for example, in preparing the altar, through participation in processions during worship, such as the procession with gifts, by painting their own pictures, and by preparing brief dramatic presentations. At the same time, Masses with children still need to provide opportunities for reflection and silent prayer, assuming that the children have been prepared to participate in them.

The priest who celebrates Masses with children should make the celebration "festive, familial, and meditative" (*DMC* 23). It is particularly important that he contribute to the creation of the proper attitude on the part of the children through "his personal preparation and his manner of acting and speaking with others" (*DMC* 23).

[2] *Gottesdienst mit Kindern, Deutscher Katechetenverein,* (Trier: Liturgical Institute, 1972).

[3] Text in *RM*, pp. 49–54.

Assuming that the basic structure is preserved, the *Directory for Masses with Children* provides for making numerous adjustments. In so doing, it also sets definite limits on the creativity of the liturgist. It permits the liturgist "to omit one or other element of the introductory rite or perhaps to expand one of the elements" (*DMC* 40). The opening prayer concluding the introductory rites, like all the presidential prayers, may be freely chosen from the texts in the Missal (*DMC* 50). The text of these prayers may be adapted to the children's ability to understand (*DMC* 51).

During the Liturgy of the Word, there must always be at least one biblical reading (*DMC* 41–42). This reading may be chosen either from the Lectionary or directly from Sacred Scripture (*DMC* 43). The National Conference of Catholic Bishops responded to this recommendation of the Directory by approving the *Lectionary for Masses with Children,* the first volume of which was published in 1993.[4]

A pastoral introduction is also provided. Like the *Directory for Masses with Children,* it provides that children may also participate in presenting the readings. Suitable texts may also be read, with various children taking different roles. When an introduction to the biblical readings is desired, nonbiblical readings, stories, or even showing and explaining appropriate pictures may be used for this purpose. The interpretation of the texts that have been presented may take place not only through the homily but also through conversation with the children, through a dramatic scene (a catechetical play), or by explaining self-made pictures related to the special theme of the readings. This interpretation of the word of God may also be presented by parents, catechists, or teachers. The children should always participate in the psalms, songs in the form of psalmody, or the *Alleluias* that are sung between the readings.

[4] Three-volume set published by The Liturgical Press: Cycle B (Sundays and Weekdays), 1993; Cycle C (Sundays and Weekdays), 1994; Cycle A (Sundays and Weekdays), 1995. Four-volume set (Cycles A, B, C, and Weekdays) under the Pueblo Books imprint also published by The Liturgical Press.

Children participate in the preparation of the gifts, as previously discussed (above, p. 124), as part of preparing the altar and the procession with gifts.

The three versions of the Eucharistic Prayer published by the Congregation for Sacred Worship on November 1, 1974, may be used.[5] These prayers contain all the important elements of the Eucharistic Prayer, as described by the General Instruction (*GIRM* 55). These Eucharistic Prayers for use with children have been shortened and reformulated in language suitable for children. In order to promote the active participation of the children, the number of acclamations has been increased.

The first of these Eucharistic Prayers strongly emphasizes the theme of "God, our Father" and is especially easy to understand. The second prayer ("God, our loving Father") provides the most opportunities for the children to actively participate. The third ("We thank you, God our Father") contains many alternate sections that may be included between the opening dialogue and the text of the preface, after the post-*Sanctus*, and again after the epiclesis asking for the fruits of Communion. In spite of the simplicity of the language, the editors did not fall prey to the danger of "infantilism."

In dealing with the Communion rite, the Directory emphasizes that certain elements are important and may not be omitted: the Our Father, the breaking of the bread, and the invitation to receive Communion (*DMC* 53). In regard to the concluding rites, great value is to be placed on saying a few words before the blessing. These comments should especially focus on "the connection between the liturgy and life" (*DMC* 54). The blessing should always close with the Trinitarian formula and the sign of the cross.

It is taken for granted that great value is also laid on the style of music and singing. Especially on solemn festivals, this may involve children's choirs, with the children playing musical instruments suited to them and especially songs that children like to sing.

[5] *RM*, pp. 1123–1138.

The situation of young people today is such that pastors must be much more concerned about them than in earlier centuries. More than fifteen years ago, a synod held at Würzburg, Germany, approved a decree dealing especially with problems associated with Masses with youth. Part of this decree reads as follows:

"Given the present situation in society and in the Church, adolescents and young people do not easily find access to worship. . . . The number of young people who experience no support either from their home or from the general atmosphere is constantly increasing. Neither family prayer nor attendance of the whole family at worship is part of their experience. Others stay away, either because they are influenced by their non-Christian environment or in reaction to forms of faith that they experienced in their own family. The milieu of school, college, and the world of work has called the faith of many young people into question. Even more have experienced a period in which they were personally skeptical of the faith. All this contributes to the fact that many young people see themselves obligated to participate in worship as a duty that is paralyzed by ancient traditions. Its language and symbols are difficult to understand and their meaning unclear. Many say: We do not find the real problems of the world and the questions of people today, especially since the usual forms of worship do not allow for any personal contribution of the participants."[6]

These realities explain the special conditions that young believers confront and their psychological situation, and why those engaged in the pastoral care of youth must do everything possible to take these realities into account in ministering to young people. These efforts are already supported and encouraged by the Constitution on the Sacred Liturgy when it states that training in liturgy should take the age, situation, style of life, and degree of religious development and understanding into account (SC 19; 34). It also says: "Provided that the substantial unity of the Roman rite is preserved, provision shall be made . . . for legitimate variations and adaptations to different groups, regions and peoples" (SC 38).

---

[6] *Gemeinsame Synode,* 4.2.1.6, p. 209.

In dealing with Masses with youth, two viewpoints deserve special consideration. With all consideration for the psychological condition of youth and the way in which their spirituality is influenced by contemporary realities, the deepest nature of the Eucharistic celebration should never be hidden or falsified. This celebration is always our encounter with the unique saving act of the triune God. The Eucharist reaches its high point in the Son's sacrificial offering of himself to the Father's saving will, and we who participate also permit ourselves to become part of this offering. These realities should never be obscured or watered down. It would be better not to celebrate the Eucharist at all than to do so in a way that does not deserve to be called Eucharist.

The second viewpoint deals with the relationship of youth to the parish Mass. Masses with young people should not result in their being isolated from the assembly but should rather lead them into participating in and supporting parish worship. This presupposes that the adults in the parish cultivate and work together with young people in a spirit of mutual trust. This includes involving the young in the preparations for and the celebration of parish worship and in the main service of the parish as well.[7]

Such community should also be created in the rest of parish life and will enrich the whole parish. The Würzburg Synod expressed this conviction:

"Children and young people all have their own gifts and tasks in edifying the community, just as every Christian and every group in the Church does. For this reason the provision of worship services with children and youth should not be viewed simply as an accommodation of these groups. Rather, the community must be thankful for the enrichment of its life which results from the participation of children and young people. The openness and joy of children, the spontaneity and the critical awareness of young people, as well as their willingness to become involved in any project that they recognize as meaningful and their thankfulness for the experience of being accepted are valuable to all. Thus chil-

[7] *Gemeinsame Synode*, 4.2.3.2., pp. 211f.

dren and young people can bring new life into the community's worship that will benefit all the faithful."[8]

MASSES WITH SMALL GROUPS

While the General Instruction for the most part concerned itself only with the celebration of the parish Mass, the Congregation for Divine Worship issued its instruction *Actio Pastoralis* already on May 15, 1969.[9] This instruction contains specific guidelines for Masses with special groups and fellowships, including smaller groups. This document establishes the validity and pastoral significance of such Masses and takes the special realities of individual groups into account.

On the basis of this and related general regulations of the General Instruction (see above, pp. 123f.), the German Conference of Bishops issued its guidelines for Masses with small groups.[10] They were adopted throughout the German-speaking territories. Switzerland was an exception, since the Swiss bishops published their own instructions, which were published in 1971 together with a manual prepared by the Swiss Liturgical Commission.[11] The following discussion is based on the guidelines of the German Conference of Bishops.

These small fellowships may be various kinds of groups: families, groups of neighbors, apostolates, youth groups, participants and guests at conferences, marriages, jubilees, funerals, school classes, and finally, even small groups that gather around a sick person. In such Masses, which are also known as Masses with small groups and Masses in the home, the structure of the parish Mass is to be preserved. Care is also to be taken that they do not result in isolation from the larger parish but rather that they facilitate access to it:

---

[8] Ibid., 4.3., p. 212.

[9] *DOL*, pp. 672–676.

[10] *Richtlinien für Messfeiern kleiner Gemeinschaften (Gruppenmessen)*, in *Nachkonziliare Dokumentation* (Trier: Liturgical Institute, 1970), nos. 31, 43–47.

[11] *Messfeier für bestimmte Personenkreise* (Zürich: Liturgical Institute, 1971).

"Since a Mass with a small group makes it possible to directly experience the basic structure of the Eucharistic celebration, such a Mass can result in a deepened understanding of the Eucharistic celebration in a much larger context, for example, the parish Mass on Sunday. When we are part of a larger assembly, it is possible to feel that we are anonymous; this anonymity will then be found to be less of a burden. The celebration of the Mass with a small group should thus assist individuals more easily to find their places in the larger fellowship."[12]

Ordinarily such Masses with small groups should be celebrated only on weekdays.

The place in which such Masses are celebrated is preferably either a small liturgical space (for example, a chapel or a church used only on weekdays) or even a suitably arranged living room or assembly room. It is also possible to use a sickroom or a home for the elderly. In nonliturgical spaces a festively decorated table may serve as the altar. Liturgical vessels such as the paten and chalice should not be dispensed with. It is taken for granted that the dress and attitude of the participants are dignified as befits the Eucharist. The priest must be recognizable as the representative of Christ and the president of the Eucharistic assembly. The priest should therefore not forgo the use of liturgical vestments. "In unusual circumstances, the priest may be identified as a priest in the same way as in the administration of other sacraments. It is taken for granted that the stole will never be missing."[13]

As far as the form of the Eucharistic celebration is concerned, the guidelines specify a careful choice of prayers, readings, and songs, corresponding to the individual situation and the ability of the participants to understand. This also applies to the formulation of the prayers, which, however, never may ignore the basic ideas of the pattern. Since the purpose of the introductory rites is "that the faithful coming together take on the form of a community and prepare themselves to listen to God's word and celebrate the eucharist properly" (*GIRM* 24), it may be that "these presupposi-

[12] *Richtlinien für Messfeiern kleiner Gemeinschaften.*
[13] Ibid., II, 2.

tions have already been achieved through associations with one another that precede the eucharistic celebration."[14]

In services of the Word the biblical readings may not be replaced by nonbiblical readings. Members of the group may participate in their selection. One of the readings chosen must also be a reading from the Gospels. Silent meditation may take the place of the chants between the readings. The homily may be replaced by a spiritual conversation. Intercessions may be formulated and presented by the participants themselves.

The participants should also take an active role in the preparation of the gifts. Before the preface those who participate in the celebration may express their own personal reasons for giving thanks. The rites of breaking the bread and drinking from the chalice are particularly easy to perform in a small group and have great symbolic power. Before the closing prayer the participants may add their own prayers spoken from the heart and expressing their own experience of the Eucharistic celebration.

The expanded texts of the final blessing are especially useful. "If an agape meal is to follow, it should be clearly differentiated from the preceding eucharistic celebration."[15]

Certainly, such a Eucharist with a small group can effectively contribute to the participants' becoming of "one heart and one soul," like the early congregation in Jerusalem.

"It is not at all unusual that these Masses, with their experience of a clearly defined fellowship, open new doors to the understanding of the Eucharist. Such fellowship in the family of God can be directly experienced, and the individual can take an active part in shaping the service. Silence and meditation, a dialogue sermon, and the confession of faith often make it clear that our service of worship of God is also God's service to us. In surprising ways we experience that God wills to give us joy and peace, safety and confidence, hope and comfort, and that he can do it."[16]

[14] Ibid., II, 3.
[15] Ibid., II, 3 (last sentence).
[16] *Gemeinsame Synode*, 3, 2., p. 207.

Chapter Four

Sunday and the Eucharistic Celebration

The Second Vatican Council raised our awareness of the inner relationship between Sunday and the Eucharistic celebration in a very urgent manner. It calls Sunday the "original feast day" and "the foundation and kernel of the whole liturgical year" (*SC* 106). These assertions are based on the following:

"By a tradition handed down from the apostles, which took its origin from the very day of Christ's resurrection, the Church celebrates the paschal mystery every eighth day, which day is appropriately called the Lord's Day or Sunday. For on this day Christ's faithful are bound to come together into one place. They should listen to the word of God and take part in the Eucharist, thus calling to mind the passion, the resurrection, and the glory of the Lord Jesus, and giving thanks to God who 'has begotten them again, through the resurrection of Christ from the dead, unto a living hope' (1 Pet. 1:3)" (*SC* 106).

It is therefore all the more disappointing for those of us who followed the Council with great hope that the number of worshipers at Sunday Mass has gone down so sharply. This is confirmed by numerous statistics. This fact is partially explained by developments in society that have changed our lifestyle in ways that make it difficult to go to Mass (for example, weekend tourism, leisure time activities). On the other hand, it signals a terrifying loss of faith. People feel an inner obligation to participate in Mass only where the Eucharist is believed to be the source and summit and goal of Christian life.

More than a few base their nonattendance on the false opinion that the "Sunday obligation" is only a rule of the Church and that it is therefore not especially binding on them. Others refer to other alternatives that are supposedly equal in value to Sunday Mass, such as works of neighborly love, meetings that contribute to social causes or have cultural value, etc.; or people even assert that the cultivation of their private piety through prayer in their "chamber" or while walking about in God's impressive nature is equally as valuable.

In view of these tendencies, the following historical and theological information should be considered. For the sake of brevity, it is presented in the form of theses:

1. Sunday, which is considered the first day of the week both by Jewish and classical reckoning, plays an important role in the life of the apostolic congregations. This is an important role in terms of salvation history. Sunday is:
   a. the day of the resurrection of Jesus Christ. This, taken together with his preceding passion (the "paschal mystery") is the primal fact of the Christian faith;
   b. the day on which the Resurrected One most often appeared to his disciples;
   c. the day of the Pentecost experience, which is to be seen as the revelation and sending of the Church to carry out its mission in the power of the Holy Spirit.

2. Even at the time of the apostles, Sunday was the preferred day for the congregation to assemble for worship services. In these services, remembering the Lord through participating in the Eucharistic "table of the Lord" played a significant role (see 1 Cor 16:2; 11:17-34).

3. The first Christians took it for granted that participation in these services of worship was an essential expression of belonging to Christ. Such sharing in his body and blood (see 1 Cor 10:16f.) was also a sign of the joy they experienced in their fellowship with the risen Lord and their joyful expectation of his coming again. It was here that people experienced their fellowship as brothers and sisters who had all been redeemed and who nourished one another's faith through their mutual faithful witness.

4. Since participation in the Sunday celebration of the Eucharist was such an inner necessity of Christian existence, believers at first had no need of a commandment of the Church that made going to Mass a strict duty. The leaders of the Church needed to admonish and warn only when faith in Christ had become weak and people were on the road to apostasy. Thus toward the end of the first century, the Letter to the Hebrews says: "not neglecting to meet together, as is the habit of some, but encouraging one another, and all the more as you see the Day approaching" (Heb 10:25). The *Didache*, a writing from the end of the first century that gives us important information about the worship life of Christians, also clearly states that participation in the Sunday Eucharistic celebration was considered to be an inner obligation: "Come together on the Lord's Day, break bread, and give thanks, after you have confessed your sins so that your sacrifice may be pure" (*Didache* 14, 1).

5. Ignatius of Antioch considered the Sunday Eucharist to be the defining mark of Christians, one that differentiated them from the Jews who celebrated the Old Testament Sabbath. He even wrote to the church in Magnesia (9, 1f.) that Christians cannot live without observing the Lord's Day. What Ignatius, writing at the beginning of the second century, says is repeated again by the martyrs who lived in the North African city of Abitine at the beginning of the fourth century. In spite of being tortured and threatened with death, they said: "We cannot exist without the *dominicum* (the Sunday Lord's Supper)."

6. This Christian awareness first begins to pale as masses of people joined the Church beginning in the fourth century. Many then began to experience the Sunday Eucharistic celebration as an onerous duty, and the leaders of the Church more and more emphasized its obligatory character.

In the light of the preceding historical and theological statements, it becomes clear that the current indifference of many Christians toward the Sunday celebration of the Mass is a deadly danger for their faith and their life as Christians. Many appeal to the supposed priority of service to the world as a reason for downgrading the significance of the Sunday Eucharist. Such Christians need to be reminded that service and action on behalf of the world and society quickly run out into the sand and dry up if they are not continually nourished by Christ's love. The source of this experience of Christ's love is given to us primarily in the Eucharist, in which we are caught up into Christ's offering of himself to the Father. The goal of the so-called Sunday obligation is to open the fount of Christ's love and let it flow freely. For this reason this duty should not be considered as merely one of many commandments of the Church, but rather as the necessary inner result of Christ's offering of himself for us.